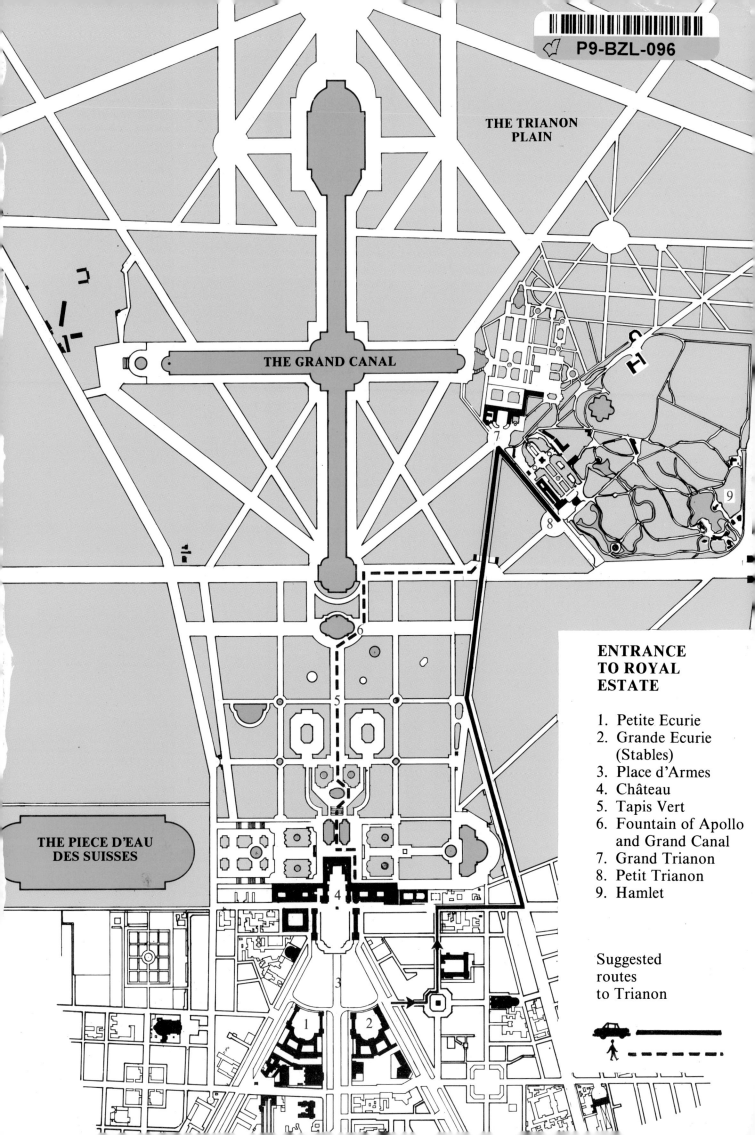

P9-BZL-096

THE TRIANON
PLAIN

THE GRAND CANAL

THE PIECE D'EAU
DES SUISSES

**ENTRANCE
TO ROYAL
ESTATE**

1. Petite Ecurie
2. Grande Ecurie
   (Stables)
3. Place d'Armes
4. Château
5. Tapis Vert
6. Fountain of Apollo
   and Grand Canal
7. Grand Trianon
8. Petit Trianon
9. Hamlet

Suggested
routes
to Trianon

CONTENTS

(*) MAPS AND FLOORPLANS

Information

The Château is open from 9.45 am to 5pm and closed on Mondays and holidays.

Art lovers will need several days in order to fully appreciate all of the royal domain of Versailles.
Visitors with only a few hours on their hands may choose any of the various guided tours organized by the *Bureau d'Action Culturelle* (39 50 58 32).

Photographies : Jacques GIRARD
Jean-Claude VARGA
Bernard DUPONT, René-Paul PAYE
Plans : Dominique TOUZOT
Hervé JACQUES
Pierre BEQUET, Michel LEFEBVRE
Maquette : Pierre KEGELS
Photogravure :
BUSSIERE ARTS GRAPHIQUES
Ateliers PERENCHIO
et PHAG-PARIS
Photocomposition :
S.P.V. - Versailles
Achevé d'imprimer le 15 Juin 198
par B.E. Impression
Imprimeur à Paris
Dépôt légal 2e trimestre 1988
Copyright : Editions d'Art Lys
ISBN 2-85495-016-X

VERSAILLES

DANIEL MEYER

*Conservateur au Musée National
des Châteaux de Versailles et de Trianon*

Translated by Sylvie KLEINMAN

CHRONOLOGY

1624 Louis XIII has a hunting lodge built on the hill of Versailles.

1631 Louis XIII commissions Philibert Le Roy to build a small château on the site of the hunting lodge.

1660 Louis XIV weds Maria-Theresa, Infanta of Spain, on June 7.
The couple take up residence at Versailles on October 25.

1661 Cardinal Mazarin, the prime minister, dies.
Beginning of Louis XIV's personal reign.
Colbert is appointed Superintendent of Finances.
Birth of the Grand Dauphin.

1663 The architect Le Vau builds the first orangery and begins work on the Menagerie.

1664 "Pleasures of the Enchanted Island", an entertainment presented by the king, is held in May.

1665 The first statues are put up in the gardens.
The Grotto of Tethys is created.

1667 Work begins on the Grand Canal.

1668 Le Vau's project to enlarge the part of the château facing the gardens with an "enveloppe de pierre" is approved.
Louis XIV offers a "Great Royal Entertainment" to a bewildered Court on July 18.

1670 The Trianon de Porcelaine is built.

1672 Work begins on the Bath Apartment and the Ambassadors' Staircase.

1674 24 statues are commissioned for the gardens.
The last of the three great entertainments held at Versailles is given by Louis XIV.
Hardouin-Mansart begins enlargement of château ; the terrace facing the gardens is replaced by the Hall of Mirrors.

1678 Le Brun completes the decoration of the State Apartments.

1682 Following a royal decree on May 6, Versailles becomes the official residence of the Court and seat of the government.

1684 The Hall of Mirrors is completed and the Orangery built.

1685 Work begins on the North Wing.

1687 The Marble Trianon is built.

1689 Louis XIV orders his silverware and silver furniture to be melted down in December.

1710 The Royal Chapel is completed.
The Duc d'Anjou, third son of the Duc de Bourgogne and the future Louis XV, is born on February 15.

1715 Louis XIV dies on September 1st.
Louis XV leaves Versailles for Vincennes on September 9.

1722 Louis XV once again takes up residence at Versailles on June 15.

1725 Louis XV weds Marie-Leczinska, daughter of King Stanislas of Poland, in Fontainebleau on September 5.

1738 Major changes are undertaken in Private Apartments.

1747 Marriage of the Dauphin to Maria-Josepha of Saxony.

1754 Birth of the Duc de Berry, future Louis XIV, on August 23.

1768 Gabriel completes the Petit Trianon.

1770 The Dauphin weds Marie-Antoinette, Archduchess of Austria and Lorraine on May 16.
Inauguration of the Royal Opera built by Gabriel.

1771 Project to rebuild the façades of the château facing the town.
Gabriel begins work on the Louis XV Wing.

1774 Louis XV dies of smallpox at Versailles on May 10.

1783 Treaty is signed ending the American War of Independence.
The Queen's Hamlet is built at Trianon.

1789 Opening session of the States General in the *Salle des Menus Plaisirs* on May 5.
The King, Royal Family and Court leave Versailles for Paris after the mob invades the château on October 6, never to return.

1792 The *Convention* orders the sale of the royal furniture following a proposal put forth by the *député* Roland on October 20.

1793 Louis XVI is condemned to death and guillotined on January 21st.
Marie-Antoinette is beheaded on October 16.

1814 Louis XVIII orders that the château's apartments be "restored and made liveable".

1833 On September 1st, Louis-Philippe orders that the château of Versailles be transformed into a Museum of French History.

1837 The Museum of Versailles is inaugurated on June 10.

1871 The king of Prussia is proclaimed emperor of Germany in the Hall of Mirrors on January 18.
With the onset of the Commune in March, the National Assembly moves to Versailles to sit in the Royal Opera.

1919 The Treaty of Versailles ending World War I is signed in the Hall of Mirrors on June 28.

1957 The Royal Opera, entirely restored, is opened to the public.

1962 General de Gaulle, president of France, decides to restore and refurnish the Grand Trianon.

1975 The Queen's Bedchamber is restored.

1978 The Consulate and Empire Rooms are reopened.

1980 Original furniture is returned to the King's Bedchamber and the Hall of Mirrors.

1984 The staircase designed by Gabriel is built.

1986 The Attic rooms of the History of French Museum are reopened.
The *Galerie Basse* and 18th-century rooms are restored on the ground floor of the main building.

INTRODUCTION

The name Versailles is known around the world as that of the vastest and most luxurious château ever built by a king. To the visitor with little knowledge of the ins and outs of French history, the names of Louis XIV and Marie-Antoinette are linked, often casting aside the other kings, queens and princes who lived here. Certain authors, striving for excessive symbolism only created with hindsight, have at times tried to explain Versailles as a representation of the myth of the sun, under the pretext that Louis XIV was known as the Sun King (as were several of his ancestors), and that his bedchamber had been placed in the geometric center of the château (this fact owing to an oversight during the conversion of the royal apartments in 1701).

In fact the importance of Versailles and those who lived there should be explained otherwise. Rather than a solar symbol, Versailles stood for the *Ancien Régime*, or so-called absolute monarchy, a force which it would be more appropriate to term as one of divine and individual right.

Curiously enough, it was in a hunting lodge at Versailles, soon to be replaced by a small château, that in 1630 on the *"Journée des Dupes"* (Day of the Duped) Louis XIII confirmed the rights of Cardinal Richelieu, already engrossing power like the first king to hunt in the woods at Versailles, Henri IV ; and it was at Versailles that the States General met for the last time in 1789, marking the beginning of the end for the ancient line of the Capetians, who had ruled over France since AD 987.

Between 1630 and 1789 the château grew in size, its gardens were laid out and a new town was built. Louis XIV made Louis XIII's hunting lodge into a bigger and bigger and more and more luxurious country residence until, in April of 1682, he decided to make Versailles the seat of his government. During those years his architects, first Levau then Hardouin-Mansart, his painter Lebrun and his gardener Le Nôtre had left their mark. But the king's influence had been decisive : from his mother, Anne of Austria, his grandmother Marie de Médicis and his ancestor Marguerite de Valois (sister of François I), he had inherited a taste for the plastic arts. From his father Louis XIII, whom he had hardly known and of which little was said, he had a taste for music and sound government, a principle defended by almost all his ancestors since the creation of the French monarchy.

His grandson Louis XV succeeded him in 1716, and though he only decided to transform the château's architecture at the end of his reign, in 1770, he nonetheless inherited his ancestor's taste for the arts, as can be seen in his private apartments. He took after his Italian ancestors, the Medici or House of Savoy, regarding secrecy in politics as essential, and it was, in fact, in his private apartments — far from the Court's lack of discretion —that the *Bien-Aimé* ("beloved") took some of his most important decisions. But neither did he neglect etiquette, the rules of which had been set down by his predecessors, nor family life of which he was reminded at times by a somewhat neglected wife, and in particular by his daughters of whom he was especially fond.

Finally Louis XVI, grandson and heir to Louis XV whose reign was inopportunely cut short by the Revolution, had inherited herculean strength from his grandfather Augustus of Saxony, King of Poland. From his ancestors of the House of Bourbon he got not only a taste for hunting, but also a genuine interest in science. By his side Marie-Antoinette, daughter of the former Duc de Lorraine crowned emperor and therefore great-granddaughter of Louis XIV's brother *Monsieur*, Philippe Duc d'Orléans and the famous Princess Palatine, left on Versailles the mark of her love for music and theater which she had acquired from the Habsburgs of Austria as well as from Louis XIII.

Much more than just a history of 17th and 18th-century art, a visit to Versailles will leave the visitor with a broader image of France's past.

ATTIC STOREYS

1 Ceiling of
 the 1830 Room
2 Skylight of the Hall
 of Battles
3 South Attic - Museum of
 History : the 1st Empire
4 Ceiling of
 the Coronation Room
5 The Queen's
 Private Cabinet -
 cont'd (mezzanine)
6 Chimay Attic - Museum
 of History : Revolution,
 Directoire, Consulate
7 Ceiling of
 the Hall of Mirrors
8 The King's Private
 Apartments (upper level)
9 Madame de
 Pompadour's Apartment
10 Madame du Barry's
 Apartment

11 Monsieur de Maurepas'
 Apartment
12 Ceiling of
 the Hercules Room
13 Ceiling of the
 Chapel Vestibule
14 Museum of
 History :
 the 19th Century
15 The Prince de Beauvau's
 Apartment

PLAN OF
THE CHATEAU

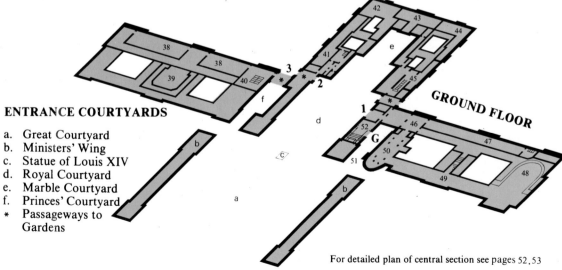

FIRST FLOOR   For detailed plan of central section see pages 12 . 13

16 1830 Room
17 Hall of Battles
18 Congress Room
19 Upper landing of Princes'
 Staircase
20 1792 Room
21 Madame de Maintenon's
 Apartment
22 Coronation Room
23 Loggia of the Queen's
 Staircase
24 The Queen's Apartment
25 The Queen's Private
 Cabinets
26 The King's Apartment
27 Hall of Mirrors
 War Drawing Room
 Peace Drawing Room
28 State Apartment

29 The King's Private Suite
30 Hercules Room
31 Upper Chapel Vestibule
32 17th Century Rooms
33 Questel Staircase
 and access to
 the Royal Opera Box
34 The Royal Opera
35 19th Century Rooms
36 Chapel Gallery
37 Upper landing of
 the Gabriel Staircase

ENTRANCE COURTYARDS

a. Great Courtyard
b. Ministers' Wing
c. Statue of Louis XIV
d. Royal Courtyard
e. Marble Courtyard
f. Princes' Courtyard
* Passageways to
 Gardens

GROUND FLOOR

38 Napoleonic Rooms
 The Consulate
 and the Empire
39 Congress Room
40 Princes' Staircase
41 The Dauphine's
 Apartment
42 The Dauphin's
 Apartment
43 Lower Gallery
 Central Vestibule
 Marie-Antoinette's
 Apartment
44 Madame Victoire's
 Apartment
45 Madame Adelaide's
 Apartment
46 Lower Chapel
 Vestibule
47 17th Century Rooms
48 Opera parterre
49 Crusades Room
50 Royal Chapel
51 Chapel Courtyard
52 Gabriel Staircase

For detailed plan of central section see pages 52 . 53

1-2-3-G   ENTRANCES TO CHATEAU

The Courtyards

After walking past the *Grande* and *Petite Écuries* (Stables) and crossing the *Place d'Armes* (Royal Parade Ground) visitors enter the Great Courtyard of the château through the gateway crowned with the arms of France. To the right and left are two long buildings with double-sloped or mansard rooves ; they are known as the Ministers' Wings, recalling the fact that Versailles was the capital of France from 1682 to 1789. Under the *Ancien Régime* the Captain of the French Guards had his quarters in the far pavilions of these wings to the left, and the Commander of the Swiss Guards to the right.

The equestrian statue of Louis XIV (1837) marks the spot where, up until the Revolution, a gate separated the two courtyards. The Royal Courtyard is flanked on the right by a stone wing which contrasts with the pink and white harmony of the other buildings. Built by Gabriel at the end of the 18th century, it is the only part of the transformation work planned at the end of Louis XV's reign and under Louis XIV to have been completed. Opposite stands the Dufour Pavillon, built in the 19th century to achieve symmetry, but without replacing the old wing, a remainder of the buildings which ran along the Royal Courtyard from 1662 to 1771, and housed some of the King's councils as well as the palace's government.

Through the gilt railings further on, wings open onto the Queen's Staircase and the vestibule of the former Ambassador's Staircase. The richer architecture of the busts on the consoles heralds the décor of the buildings surrounding the Marble Courtyard.

The Marble Courtyard, recently raised to its original level, is the same size as the courtyard of Louis XIII's little château. The balcony in the centre leads into the king's bedchamber. Above the windows the clock on the pediment was at one time set at the hour of death of the preceding king ; in fact, this only applied to the deaths of Louis XIV in 1715 and Louis XV in 1774.

▲
THE MARBLE COURTYARD

◀ THE LOUIS XV WING AND THE CHAPEL

The north wing and 17th-century rooms

The ground floor and first storey of the north wing are toured before the state apartments as a sort of introduction to help visitors gain better knowledge of French history under the first three kings of the House of Bourbon, Henri IV, Louis XIII and Louis XIV. It was Henri IV who was the first to come hunt in the game-filled forests of Versailles. His son Louis XIII had a small hunting lodge built there ; its proportions remain at the heart of Louis XIV's immense palace. Portraits and busts of kings, princes, dignitaries and artists, as well as scenes of

The Musée de l'Histoire de France also includes the Crusades Rooms and 19th-century Rooms in the North Wing. Those dealing with the 17th century take up two floors facing the gardens.

▲
17TH-CENTURY ROOMS,
SECOND FLOOR OF NORTH WING

VERSAILLES IN 1668
BY PIERRE PATEL ▶

royal homes, civilian and especially military life, provide insight into the monarchy, shown here in its prime.

These rooms also preserve the feeling of the museum created by Louis-Philippe to commemorate France's glory, even though works carried out at a later date than the events depicted here have been removed.

◄ LOUIS XIV, PATRON OF SCIENCE, BY TESTELIN

The Chapel

Built between 1699 and 1709, the chapel was the last bit of construction built under Louis XIV at Versailles, and is the work of Hardouin-Mansart and Robert de Cotte. Its high silhouette, especially on the side facing the gardens, breaks up the horizontal uniformity of the château's buildings, a bit like the Sainte Chapelle in Paris which it resembles by its Palatinate-type (or two-storeyed) architecture, with an upper chapel (here only made up of the galleries) and a lower chapel.

Dedicated to Saint-Louis, ancestor and patron saint of the royal French family, it is the château's fifth chapel and was consecrated on June 5 1710 by Cardinal de Noailles. The décor, and especially the ceiling paintings, depict the link between the Old and New Testaments characterizing the spirit of Christianity, thanks to the Mystery of the Holy Trinity painted by Jouvenet, Coypel and Lafosse. The side chapels are dedicated to patron saints of the royal family, and the organ loft, with its portrayal of King David,

THE CHAPEL
◄ THE ALTAR AND ORGAN LOFT

symbolizes the moral affinity which existed between the Hebrew kings and the sovereigns of France.

The upper chapel vestibule, or chapel drawing room, is level with the royal gallery and the State Apartment which it links ; it praises the king with two statues representing Glory holding a medallion of Louis XV by Vassé, and royal magnanimity by Bousseau.

▲
THE CHAPEL CEILING

◄ THE UPPER CHAPEL VESTIBULE

11

FIRST FLOOR

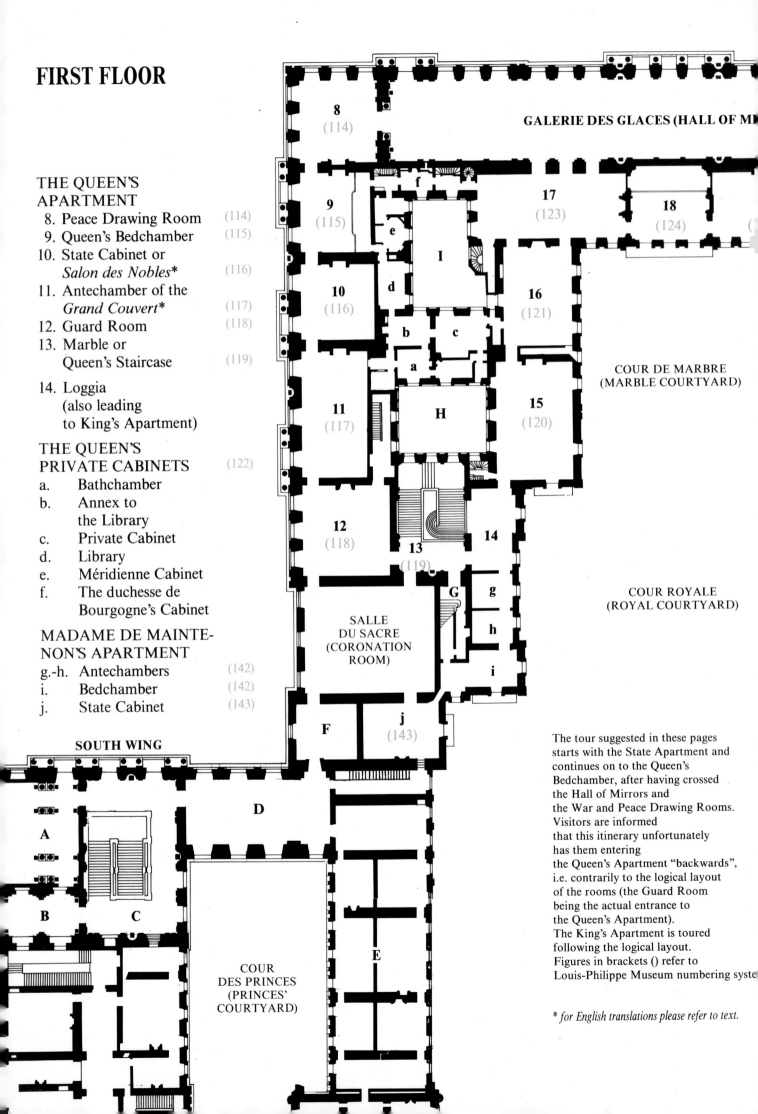

THE QUEEN'S APARTMENT
- 8. Peace Drawing Room (114)
- 9. Queen's Bedchamber (115)
- 10. State Cabinet or *Salon des Nobles** (116)
- 11. Antechamber of the *Grand Couvert** (117)
- 12. Guard Room (118)
- 13. Marble or Queen's Staircase (119)
- 14. Loggia (also leading to King's Apartment)

THE QUEEN'S PRIVATE CABINETS (122)
- a. Bathchamber
- b. Annex to the Library
- c. Private Cabinet
- d. Library
- e. Méridienne Cabinet
- f. The duchesse de Bourgogne's Cabinet

MADAME DE MAINTENON'S APARTMENT
- g.-h. Antechambers (142)
- i. Bedchamber (142)
- j. State Cabinet (143)

SOUTH WING

GALERIE DES GLACES (HALL OF M|

8 (114)

9 (115)

10 (116)

11 (117)

12 (118)

13 (119)

14

17 (123)

18 (124)

16 (121)

15 (120)

f

e

d

I

b

c

a

H

g

h

i

G

j (143)

F

SALLE DU SACRE (CORONATION ROOM)

COUR DE MARBRE (MARBLE COURTYARD)

COUR ROYALE (ROYAL COURTYARD)

A

B

C

D

E

COUR DES PRINCES (PRINCES' COURTYARD)

The tour suggested in these pages starts with the State Apartment and continues on to the Queen's Bedchamber, after having crossed the Hall of Mirrors and the War and Peace Drawing Rooms. Visitors are informed that this itinerary unfortunately has them entering the Queen's Apartment "backwards", i.e. contrarily to the logical layout of the rooms (the Guard Room being the actual entrance to the Queen's Apartment). The King's Apartment is toured following the logical layout. Figures in brackets () refer to Louis-Philippe Museum numbering syste

for English translations please refer to text.

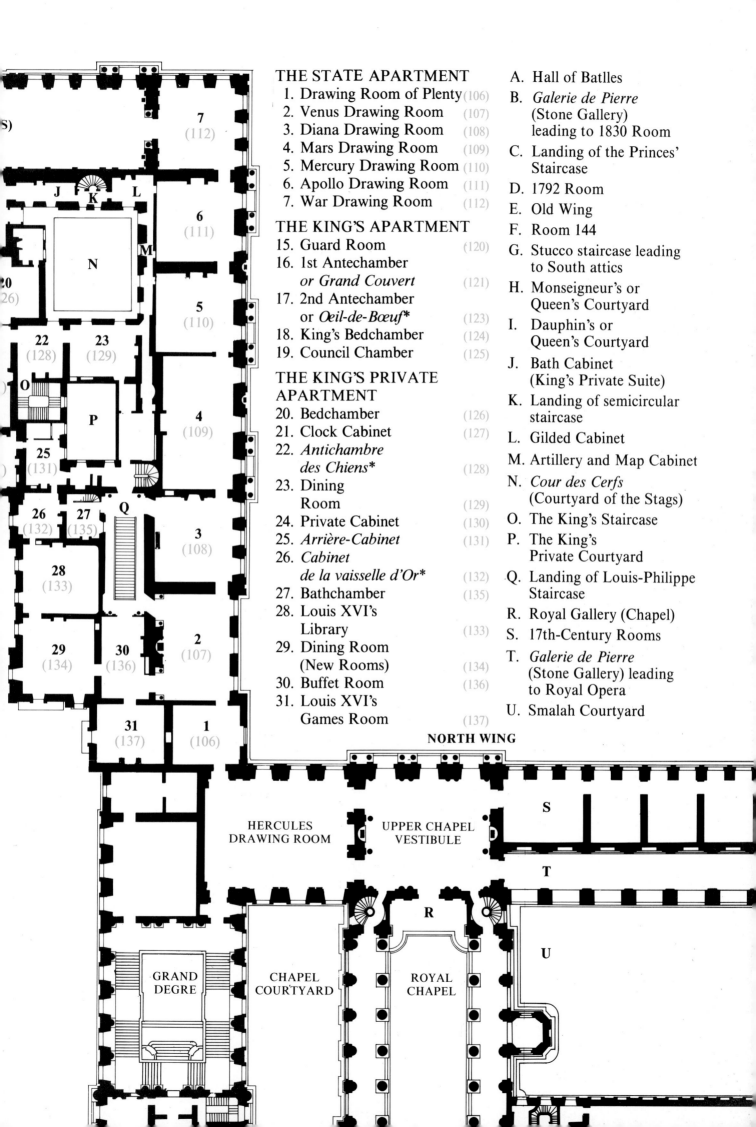

THE STATE APARTMENT
1. Drawing Room of Plenty (106)
2. Venus Drawing Room (107)
3. Diana Drawing Room (108)
4. Mars Drawing Room (109)
5. Mercury Drawing Room (110)
6. Apollo Drawing Room (111)
7. War Drawing Room (112)

THE KING'S APARTMENT
15. Guard Room (120)
16. 1st Antechamber
    or Grand Couvert (121)
17. 2nd Antechamber
    or Œil-de-Bœuf* (123)
18. King's Bedchamber (124)
19. Council Chamber (125)

THE KING'S PRIVATE APARTMENT
20. Bedchamber (126)
21. Clock Cabinet (127)
22. *Antichambre
    des Chiens** (128)
23. Dining
    Room (129)
24. Private Cabinet (130)
25. *Arrière-Cabinet* (131)
26. *Cabinet
    de la vaisselle d'Or** (132)
27. Bathchamber (135)
28. Louis XVI's
    Library (133)
29. Dining Room
    (New Rooms) (134)
30. Buffet Room (136)
31. Louis XVI's
    Games Room (137)

A. Hall of Batlles
B. *Galerie de Pierre*
   (Stone Gallery)
   leading to 1830 Room
C. Landing of the Princes'
   Staircase
D. 1792 Room
E. Old Wing
F. Room 144
G. Stucco staircase leading
   to South attics
H. Monseigneur's or
   Queen's Courtyard
I. Dauphin's or
   Queen's Courtyard
J. Bath Cabinet
   (King's Private Suite)
K. Landing of semicircular
   staircase
L. Gilded Cabinet
M. Artillery and Map Cabinet
N. *Cour des Cerfs*
   (Courtyard of the Stags)
O. The King's Staircase
P. The King's
   Private Courtyard
Q. Landing of Louis-Philippe
   Staircase
R. Royal Gallery (Chapel)
S. 17th-Century Rooms
T. *Galerie de Pierre*
   (Stone Gallery) leading
   to Royal Opera
U. Smalah Courtyard

NORTH WING

HERCULES
DRAWING ROOM

UPPER CHAPEL
VESTIBULE

GRAND
DEGRE

CHAPEL
COURTYARD

ROYAL
CHAPEL

The Grand Escalier

While reconstructing the north wing of the Royal Courtyard, the architect Gabriel had planned a main staircase to replace the Ambassadors' Staircase, pulled down in 1752, and the presence of which was sorely lacking. The framework and décor of the stairwell were built, but the steps themselves never were. The space was used as a

◀ THE GRAND ESCALIER, LOUIS XV WING

The Hercules Drawing Room

theater, but Louis-Philippe found it antiquated and had it destroyed when he restored Versailles. Since then only temporary work was done here, and it seemed fitting, in our time, to complete a project the plans of which were known but the bulk of which had never been fully carried out. This staircase is therefore new, but was built in keeping with the plans of Louis XIV's great architect.

The Hercules drawing room is the first to be visited in the State Apartment, but was the last to be built in the chateau's suite of state rooms, and stands on the site of the fourth chapel. It was designed under Louis XIV to serve as a setting for Veronese's painting "Meal at the House of Simon", a gift from the Republic of Venice to the French king in 1664. The fireplace is ornamented with magnificent chased gilt bronzes by Vassé ; above hangs another painting by Veronese, "Eliezer and Rebecca".

This room was started in 1712 by Robert de Cotte who wished to match the various types of marble (Sarrancolin, Antin, Rance) to the color schemes of the paintings. Work was interrupted in 1715 by the death of Louis XIV, and only resumed in 1725. It was completed between 1733 and 1736 when Lemoine painted the fine ceiling depicting the deification of Hercules, which gave the room its name.

Due to its considerable size (60 ft. long, 45 ft. wide and 37 ft. high), the room was used under the *Ancien Régime* for concerts, full-dress balls and official banquets, such as the *grand couvert* given in 1769 for the wedding of the duc de Chartres, father of the future king Louis-Philippe who was to restore Versailles in the 19th century.

▲
THE HERCULES
DRAWING ROOM

OVERLEAF : THE HERCULES DRAWING ROOM, DETAIL OF THE CEILING
AND MEAL AT THE HOUSE OF SIMON BY VERONESE, ON SOUTH WALL ▶

THE STATE APARTMENT

Visitors enter the State Apartment after crossing the Hercules drawing room as an introduction. This suite was altered several times before reaching its final appearance between 1671 and 1681, thanks to work supervised by Lebrun. The king lived here until 1682 when the State Apartment became a suite of drawing rooms used for Court ceremonies and entertainment. These festivities became known as *"Appartement"* evenings due to their setting, and were held by the king on Mondays, Wednesdays and Thursdays. Though the ceiling decoration has remained untouched since its creation, the furniture and mural decorative scheme have been changed throughout the years. The silver furniture was melted down in 1689 and furnishings were sold and dispersed during the Revolution (and the throne destroyed), following which paintings from the royal collection were transferred to the Louvre, and are still the essential part of the museum's collection.

The crimson damask wall hangings which hung here from the middle of Louis XV's reign to the end of Louis XVI's were recently reproduced, especially in the Mars, Mercury and Apollo drawing rooms. The paintings, busts and the Savonnerie carpets in particular (woven for the *Grande Galerie* in the Louvre) give an excellent idea of the extraordinary luxury to be found in this suite, and which even early on was considered to be a model of the genre by all European courts.

The Drawing Room of Plenty

Though this room was used as a buffet room for serving drinks on *Appartement* evenings, it stands alone in the State Apartment insofar as it is the only room not to be called after a planet god from ancient mythology. Its name derives from the Cabinet of Curios and Rare Objects (today Louis XIV's Games room) which stood behind the door, no longer used, facing the window. Louis XIV had gathered the most valuable pieces of his collections in this cabinet, some of which have been depicted by Houasse on the painted balustrade above, surrounding the sky over which "royal munificence" reigns.

Three portraits by Rigaud hang on the walls covered with Genoan velvet : the Grand Dauphin, son of Louis XIV, and two of his own sons, the duc d'Anjou crowned king of Spain under the name Philip V, and his older brother the duc de Bourgogne, father of Louis XV, also shown here in a painting by Van Loo.

The classical busts come from the royal collections ; the six medal cabinets were built after designs by Boulle and executed in his style.

▲
DETAIL OF CEILING

◀ THE DRAWING ROOM OF PLENTY

17

THE VENUS DRAWING ROOM
VIEW FACING THE DRAWING ROOM OF PLENTY

FALSE PERSPECTIVE
ON EAST WALL

The Venus and Diana Drawing Rooms

These two rooms served as upper vestibules to the Ambassadors' Staircase until it was pulled down in 1752. Luckily, their marble décor, which had matched that of the staircase, has been preserved. The full-length statue by Warin of Louis XIV dressed as a Roman emperor, as well as the bust of the king by Bernini in the Diana drawing room, maintain the celebration of the ruler which Lebrun had intended for the *Grand Escalier*.

The ceilings introduce depictions of the gods from ancient mythology who gave their names to the planets known in the 17th-century.

On the ceiling of the first drawing room an oval painted by Houasse portrays Venus crowned by three Graces as "the Goddess of Love subjugating the Gods and Powers";

Egypt) hangs a painting by Charles de Lafosse representing Diana saving Iphigenia. On the wall opposite hangs a painting by Blanchard which shows the goddess watching over a sleeping Endymion.

Some of the classical busts which can be seen in both the Venus and Diana drawing rooms already stood here under Louis XIV.

THE DIANA DRAWING ROOM
THE CEILING ►

famous lovers in ancient history have been portrayed in the corners of the ceiling.

The false perspectives on the side walls were painted by Jacques Rousseau, as were the trompe-l'œil statues representing Meleager and Atalanta.

Light meals were served in the Venus drawing room while the Diana drawing room was used for billiards. Louis XIV excelled at the game, and a large table (covered by a crimson velvet carpet when not in use) was set up in the middle of the room. The ceiling in the Diana drawing room was painted by Blanchard and depicts the goddess "presiding over hunting and navigation", two activities equally portrayed by Audran and Lafosse in the coves. Above the fireplace (ornamented with a bas-relief by Sarrazin of the Flight into

▲
THE DIANA DRAWING ROOM
MARBLE WINDOW RECESSES

THE DIANA
DRAWING ROOM ►

The Mars Drawing Room

This room was used, up until 1682, as a guard room, explaining the name of the room as well as the cornice adorned with helmets and war trophies, and the ceiling painting by Audran depicting the god of War on a chariot drawn by wolves.

Under Louis XIV this room was used for concerts on *Appartement* evenings, and galleries had been built for the musicians in 1684 on either side of the fireplace, but they were taken down in 1750. It was also under Louis XV that the large marquetry cabinets, which had contributed to the luxuriousness of the furnishings, were removed.

However this is the only room in the State Apartment in which efforts have been made to restore the paintings which hung here under Louis XV.

Though Veronese's "The Mystic Marriage of Saint Catherine" was replaced above the fireplace by Domenichino's "David" (formerly in the Sun King's bedroom in winter) the other paintings are the originals which hung here in the 18th century : "The Tent of Darius" by Lebrun, a period replica of Veronese's "The Pilgrims at Emmaus" and two portraits by Van Loo of Louis XV and Marie Leczinska.

The paintings above the doors come from the château of Saint-Germain-en-Laye and were painted by Simon Vouet, replacing the original works from the royal collection which are now kept in the Louvre. The doors in the back of the room are covered with portières as before.

THE MARS DRAWING ROOM ▶

The Mercury and Apollo Drawing Rooms

Were it not for the lavish ceilings in these two rooms — Mercury by Champaigne and Apollo by Lafosse — visitors would have a hard time imagining that these two rooms were the most luxurious of the king's State Apartment.

The Mercury room, first used as an antechamber, became the state bedchamber in 1682. The Apollo room was a bedchamber before becoming the Throne Room. The famous silver throne, its back eight feet high, stood here until 1689.

The present decorative scheme does not fully render the grandeur of the light fixtures, furniture and paintings by the great masters which enriched these two drawing rooms under the *Ancien Régime,* and filled visitors with admiration.

The walls, however, have been hung with crimson damask as before. Visitors can admire the automaton clock in the Mercury room presented to Louis XIV in 1706 by Antoine Morand. Of the 24 candelabra made in 1770 by Babel and Foliot for the Hall of Mirrors (for the wedding of the future Louis XVI to the Archduchess Marie-Antoinette), six original and imposing pieces can be seen in the Apollo room and give an idea of how the room had been furnished. The only original paintings from the royal collection to have been returned here are the portraits of Louis XIV (Rigaud) and Louis XVI (Callet) in the Throne Room.

▲
THE MERCURY DRAWING ROOM
THE CEILING

THE APOLLO
DRAWING ROOM ▶

THE HALL OF MIRRORS
the Drawing Rooms

Up until 1678, when construction work started on the Hall of Mirrors, the private royal apartments looked out onto the gardens, the king's room on the site of the present War drawing room, and the queen's on that of the Peace drawing room. They were linked by a terrace with a fountain in the middle, and from which one could admire the gardens which Le Nôtre was laying out ; the king was soon to write his treatise on "the Manner of Presenting the Gardens of Versailles".

Carried out by Hardouin-Mansart and Lebrun with the help of some of the most talented artists of the time, this unique part of the château is a change from the glorification of ancient heroes, and pays tribute to the military victories and political success of the king, henceforth known as *Louis le Grand*. Started in 1678 and completed in 1686, the hall, with its two drawing rooms linking the king and queen's apartments, was soon considered as a model of decorative art acclaimed throughout Europe.

The War drawing room, formerly the king's cabinet dedicated to Jupiter (the ceiling painting by Coypel was transferred to the Room of the Queen's Guard) is dedicated to Louis XIV's victories over the allied powers (the Empire, Spain and Holland) during the war with Holland and the treaty which ended it with the Peace of Nimeguen.

THE WAR
◀ DRAWING ROOM

27

One of the most glorious events of this campaign was the king's crossing of the Rhine; the ruler is portrayed here by Coysevox as a classical hero on horseback, in a large medallion supported by two prisoners in chains and above the relief of Clio, writing the king's history, also by Coysevox.

Lebrun chose to portray the history of Louis XIV in his ceiling painting in the Hall of Mirrors (he also painted the ceilings in the two drawing rooms).

The various cartouches explain the scenes depicted. Between episodes of the War of Devolution (1667-1668) and the War with Holland (1672-1678) the most glorious years of the Sun King's reign are portrayed on either side of the central panel entitled "the King Governs Alone".

Seventeen mirror-filled arches face the same number of windows looking out onto the gardens, as if to enhance the luxury of the Pyrenees marble pilasters crowned with "French order" capitals (created by Lebrun following the example of the classical orders) and the niches filled with the finest of the king's classical statues.

Under the *Ancien Régime* the hall made up a unique setting for official audiences, balls and entertainment. Today only some of the eight original classical statues have been returned; the busts of Roman emperors come from royal collections; as for the furniture, through lack of the original silver pieces (melted down in 1689) or those commissioned by Louis XV from the Slodtz, what can now be seen are replicas of the light fixtures which lit up the hall

THE HALL
OF MIRRORS ▶

28

for the wedding of the Dauphin, future Louis XVI, to the Archduchess Marie-Antoinette in 1770 (thanks to copies for the chandeliers and castings for the candlestands).

But the chandeliers did not hang here on a permanent basis, in order that the ceiling paintings be admired during the day.

The Peace drawing room is dedicated to the Peace of Nimeguen, and peace in general, as shown in the painting by Lemoine above the fireplace ; this work was only put here in 1729 and portrays a young King Louis XV offering his little twin daughters Henriette and Elisabeth as a pledge to peace. It was built on the site of the former Queen's Cabinet and was entirely linked to the Queen's Apartment at the beginning of the 18th century ; when there was no queen the Dauphine occupied the apartment.

At the time this drawing room was a busy *salon* and was called the Queen's Games Room. Of the original furnishings the only pieces which remain are the andirons by Boizot, Thomire and Forestier, which Marie-Antoinette had ordered for the fireplace in 1786.

At the time the queen had thought of having the room redesigned, as she found it too formal and old fashioned. The Lebrun ceiling would have been replaced by another depicting a sky with cupids.

THE PEACE
DRAWING ROOM ▶

30

THE QUEEN'S APARTMENT

This apartment is toured starting from the Peace drawing room, in other words not in the logical order. Contrarily to the King's apartment, the arrangement of the rooms here was not changed from the time they were conceived for Marie-Thérèse to the departure of Marie-Antoinette. However each queen had alterations carried out, as she actually lived here, thus giving this suite of four large rooms overlooking the South Parterre its variety in styles, in contrast to the unity prevailing in the King's Apartment.

The Queen's Bedchamber

Of the original decoration only the panelled ceiling remains in this room in which Marie-Thérèse and the two Dauphines — the grandmother and mother of Louis XV — all died, in 1683, 1690 and 1712, respectively.

Apart from the arms of Austria and France placed in the corners of the ceiling in 1770 for Marie-Antoinette (still Dauphine at the time) and the fireplace built for her in 1786 (she had been queen since 1774), the paintings and sculpted work in this room had been commissioned for Marie Leczinska, the wife of Louis XV. From 1730 to 1735 this work was supervised first by Robert de Cotte, then the two Gabriels, father and son. The sculptures by Verberckt, Dugoulon and Goupil frame the paintings above the doors by Natoire and Troy (depicting the royal children in 1734) as well as the monochrome medallions by Boucher representing four Virtues. These pain-

tings, as well as the grisaille rose, replaced the ceiling paintings by De Sève portraying Apollo which matched those in the king's bedchamber (later the Throne Room) under Louis XIV.

The furnishings are those which enhanced the room under Marie-Antoinette. This is the "summer" décor (as opposed to the velvet or brocade "winter" décor) which filled the room when, on the morning of October 6, 1789 the revolutionary mobs forced the royal family to leave Versailles for good and take up residence in the Tuileries in Paris (where they lived until August 10, 1792, the date of the fall of the monarchy).

The silk hangings are an exact reproduction of the brocade Tours silk which had been delivered in 1786, as are the embroidered seat covers and fireplace screen. The alcove carpet and curtains are also faithful copies.

The fireplace screen, however, made by Sené in 1786, as well as the andirons made by Boizot and Thomire in 1787 and the

GLORY TAKING POSSESSION OF THE CHILDREN OF FRANCE, OVERDOOR.

THE QUEEN'S
BEDCHAMBER ▶

nets had been altered throughout the years even more than the State Apartment, and grew considerably, without, however, becoming as vast as the king's private cabinets.

Under Marie-Antoinette they extended into several rooms on a mezzanine, and included not only a billiards room and a dining room, but a genuine little apartment complete with bedchamber and bathchamber (the latter has been recently restored on the ground floor facing the Marble Courtyard). The *Méridienne* and *Grand Cabinet Intérieur,* or large private cabinet, are those which have been best preserved ; the *Méridienne,* which was created and decorated in 1781 for the Dauphin's birth, is now partially furnished with original pieces.

The bookshelves in the libraries now contain some fine works bearing the queen's arms. As for the private cabinet, entirely redecorated in 1783 by the Rousseau brothers following plans by Mique, it is now furnished with either original pieces or equivalent period furniture.

Interestingly enough, the queen had a bathchamber in her private cabinet before having one on the ground floor (which still exists). However, contrarily to Marie-Thérèse and Marie Leczinska, Marie-Antoinette never had a private chapel, and though queens gave audience ceremoniously in the state apartment, it was in the private cabinets that they received painters, musicians or writers without the need for etiquette.

jewelry cabinet built by Schwerdfeger also in 1787, are all part of the room's original furnishings. This also applies to the wall clock, with its Baillon mechanism, which was ordered for the Dauphine in 1745 but only placed here for Marie-Antoinette, and the bedspread.

The folding stools were made by Sené, and the two armchairs by Tilliard. They are authentic period pieces, but came from other royal furniture collections.

The Queen's Private Cabinets

On either side of the bed visitors will notice two doors which blend into the wall hangings. These doors lead to the *Cabinets Intérieurs,* or private cabinets ; it was to these small rooms that the queen would retire, away from the gossip and fuss of the Court. These cabi-

▲
THE MERIDIENNE,
CREATED IN 1781

THE PRIVATE
CABINET ▶

the paintings by Regnault above the doors, allegories of Sculpture and Painting.

The original 1785 furnishings include the chests and corner cupboards (Riesener), the Chinese gilt-bronze stool, the tapestry portrait of Louis XV by Cozette after Van Loo and the candelabra (Forestier).

The andirons were made from the 1786 originals ; the fireplace screen is from Compiègne, the mantel clock and matching candelabra from the boudoir of the Comte d'Artois; the stools were made by Quirinal under Napoléon but have been covered in Louis XVI style ; the chandelier is Bohemian crystal, and the Savonnerie carpet originally covered the floor of the *Galerie du Louvre*.

Apart from the queen's armchair which was never found, the furnishings gathered here help visitors imagine the type of setting in which titled ladies or ambassadors' wives were presented under the *Ancien Régime*.

The Salon des Nobles
(Room of the Queen's Gentlemen)

The ceiling of this room has remained intact, and was originally painted for Marie-Thérèse. Here — as in what was formerly the king's second antechamber in a work by Champaigne — the ceiling painted by Michel Corneille for Louis XIV's bride is an allegory to the glory of Mercury ; the god is seen spreading his influence over the Arts and Science, represented in the arches by various figures from ancient history.

The wall décoration was altered several times until reaching its final state in 1785, under Marie-Antoinette. The rich fireplace in slate-blue marble contrasts with the large panels of soberly-framed green damask and

▲
THE SALON
DES NOBLES

THE GUARD
ROOM ▶

Antechamber of the *Grand Couvert*

This antechamber, like the Mars drawing room in the King's Apartment was originally the Room of the Queen's Guard, as illustrated by the cornice and arching paintings by Paillet and Vignon depicting war themes. The center of the ceiling, however, originally painted by Vignon, has been redecorated several times ; since the second half of the 19th century it features "The Tent of Darius", inspired from the original by Lebrun in the Mars drawing room. Above the four doors (the two in the back of the room have only recently been returned) are paintings by Madeleine de Boulogne. Tapestries once covered the walls which are now hung with velvet, chosen to enhance the paintings depicting Marie-Antoinette (portrait of the queen with her children by Vigée Lebrun) and the daughters of Louis XV.

The present name of the room is derived from the fact that it was here that the king and queen dined in public, a practice known as the *Grand Couvert*. Concerts and other forms of entertainment were also given here ; before the Revolution a platform for musicians stood against the wall common with the guard room.

The Guard Room

Thanks to the functional aspect of this room (formerly one of the château's chapels) its marble decoration, completed in 1681 two years before Marie-Thérèse's death, has been preserved.

The paintings by Noël Coypel praising Jupiter's glory come from what had formerly been the king's *Grand Cabinet*, converted into the War drawing room when the Hall of Mirrors was built.

Under the *Ancien Régime* the room was cluttered with racks for the guards' arms, campbeds and sedan chairs. It was on this site that on the morning of October 6, 1789, guards lost their lives helping Marie-Antoinette seek refuge by the king's side.

▲
ABOVE : ANTECHAMBER OF THE
GRAND COUVERT

The Salle du Sacre
(Coronation room)

Until 1682 this huge room was the château's third chapel. It then served as a guard room for both king and queen for over a century.

Its décor was quite ordinary. However, owing to its considerable size, this room was the setting for major events such as the ceremony conducted on Holy Thursday during which the king would wash the feet of thirteen poor children, or the more politically crucial *Lit de Justice* on April 13 1771, by which Louis XV dismissed his parliament, leading to reforms which would have saved the monarchy were it not for the ruler's death three years later. Today the room owes its name to the painting by David depicting the coronation of Napoleon I on December 2 1804. (The first version of this masterpiece hangs in the Louvre ; the painting at Versailles was completed in 1822). Like the other works here, this painting praises the glory of the Napoleonic era, as was the wish of Louis-Philippe when he converted the château into a museum.

THE CORONATION OF NAPOLEON,
BY DAVID ▶

The Hall of Battles

This hall is reached after crossing the 1792 Room (so called because of the paintings which hang here, but which was the room of the Swiss Guards under Louis XVI) and the landing of the Princes' Staircase (so called because the fine marble staircase led to the Princes' Apartments). This huge gallery 394 feet long and 43 feet wide, takes up two storeys of the south wing (or Princes' wing) facing the gardens where the Children of France lived under the *Ancien Régime*. Its present décor dates from Louis-Philippe who had decided to gather paintings depicting some of the brilliant victories in French history. These stretch from the victory of Clovis at the battle of Tolbiac in AD 496 to the battle of Wagram won by Napoléon in 1809. Busts and bronze plaques bearing

THE GARDE NATIONALE JOINING FORCES
◀ WITH THE ARMY, BY COGNIET (1792 ROOM)

the name of princes who lost their lives in action complete this hymn to military grandeur, where the Citizen King had wished to reunite all of France's political differences.

A large room at the end of the gallery (formerly the apartment of Mademoiselle Elisabeth, sister of Louis XVI) is dedicated to the July Monarchy of 1830, when the younger branch of the House of Bourbon (the Bourbons d'Orléans) replaced the senior branch represented by Charles X, the duc d'Angoulême and the duc de Bordeaux.

From the 1830 Room visitors move on to a stone gallery which runs along the Hall of Battles, and leads to the Provence staircase (named after the brother of Louis XVI, the comte de Provence, whose apartment it led to) and the *Salle du Congrès,* built for the 1875 presidential election.

At the other end of the gallery lies the Princes' Staircase which leads to the Empire rooms on the ground floor of the south wing.

BELOW : THE HALL
OF BATTLES
▼

The Marble Staircase

The Marble Staircase, (or Queen's Staircase), built from 1679-81, matches the Ambassadors' Staircase in the King's Apartment, and leads to the Queen's Apartment ; its landing also leads to the Room of the Queen's Guard.

This staircase also gave access to the King's Apartment when, after the death of Marie-Thérèse (1683), Louis XIV had the rooms in the southwest corner of the Marble Courtyard annexed to his own new apartment.

The marble décor, the metal alloy reliefs by Le Gros and Massou above the doorways, the group of children also by Massou, and the large trompe-l'œil painting were completed in 1701 when a loggia was created, linking the King's Apartment to that of Madame de Maintenon. The proportions of the former antechamber and state cabinets were preserved when these rooms were converted for her.

Today her apartment is filled with paintings, sketches and drawings depicting the château and gardens, as well as some examples of Boulle-style furniture.

THE KING'S APARTMENT

The King's Apartment, first created in 1683, changed considerably under Louis XV with the creation of the state cabinet or Council Room (1755), and introduced a new aspect to the history and decorative scheme of Versailles.

Created shortly after the Court was set up at Versailles, the apartment expressed new conditions to be met in the king's daily life. The state apartment, henceforth the setting for festivities and ceremonies, is a separate entity from the King's Apartment proper, where rituals such as the *Lever* and *Coucher* (when the king would rise or retire in public), the *Entrées* (when privileged courtiers were allowed to enter the king's room) and the *Grand Couvert* prevailed. Here the famous *"étiquette"* reached its point of perfection. The king governed from Versailles and met with his ministers in the *Grand Cabinet*.

THE MARBLE
◀ STAIRCASE

ANTECHAMBER OF
THE OEIL DE BOEUF ▶

The décor of the King's Apartment is, in itself, an innovation. Here marble and painted ceilings are replaced by woodwork, more and more sculpted and gilded as one approaches the finest room of all, the bedchamber.

The Guard Room is the first crossed when coming from the Queen's Staircase. A battle scene by Parrocel above the fireplace is the only work to adorn the simple woodwork in this room, which was only lit by two small brass chandeliers.

The first antechamber, or *Grand Couvert,* (it was here that the king dined alone in public), is richer

than the Guard Room, and features a fine cornice and paintings by Parrocel and Bourguignon depicting military scenes. It was also here that each Monday petitions requesting favors were addressed to the king.

The second antechamber, or Antechamber of the King's Gentleman, was extended when the bedchamber was added in 1701. Until then it had been known as the *salon des Bassans,* after the painter whose works hang here. After the creation of the magnificent cornice with its bull's eye window, the room was informally called the *Oeil de Bœuf.* The cornice is decorated with figures of children at play, the work of Van Cleve, Hardy and Poulletier among others. Portraits of the royal family from the château at Saint-Cloud have replaced works by Veronese. It was in this antechamber that those courtiers privileged with an official *Entrée* waited for the king to rise in the next room.

ABOVE : ANTECHAMBER
OF THE GRAND COUVERT

41

The King's Bedchamber

This room, built in 1668, was originally a state drawing room shared by both king and queen. After the death of Marie-Thérèse it was "the room where the king dresses", and was only converted into a bedchamber in 1701 when the *Oeil de Bœuf* was enlarged.

From this date on and until the fall of the *Ancien Régime*, even after 1737 when Louis XV decided to have his bedchamber set up on the north side of the Marble Courtyard, this room was the very heart of the Court ; when the king was at Versailles it was the setting for the unfading ceremonies known as the *Lever* and *Coucher* which took place each morning and evening.

The décor is largely that of the former drawing room, with its pilasters, and paintings by Van Dyck, Caraciolo and Domenichino above the doors, and Valentin de Boulogne and Lanfranco in the attic compartments supporting the domed ceiling. The ceiling was only decorated in the 19th century when a work by Veronese was temporarily placed here. In 1701 the wall common with the Hall of Mirrors was closed off to create an alcove, crowned with a high relief by de Cousto depicting "France watching over the King's Sleep". Under Louis XIV there was only one fireplace and it was in 1761 that the two slate-blue fireplaces were added.

The furniture, which only included a bed, two armchairs and twelve folding chairs, has been recreated following inventories to resemble the summer furnishings which stood here from 1723 to 1785. The original brocade was never found, but authentic samples kept through the years made it possible to weave hangings which are a replica of those used in Marie-Antoinette's room in winter. Though designed prior to the queen's reign, they are as similar as possible to the description of those made for Louis XV. The hangings which had been placed here for Louis XIV were, following tradition, presented to the First Gentleman of the Chamber upon the king's death.

THE KING'S
◂ BEDCHAMBER

The Council Chamber

This large room, generally referred to as the Council Chamber, should more appropriately be called the King's State Cabinet. It was here that the King would summon his various councils, but also where he signed the Princes' marriage contracts, gathered his family after dinner, received congratulations or condolences, and even had titled ladies newly received at Court "presented" to him.

This vast room was only enlarged to its present size in 1755 when Louis XV decided to make two rooms — the former Council Chamber and the *Cabinet des Perruques* (Wig Cabinet) or Cabinet of Terms — into one. The magnificent sculpted panels by Jules-Antoine Rousseau (on either side of the red marble fireplace with gilt-bronze ornaments) date from that time. The paintings by Houasse above the doors originally hung in the Grand Trianon, and replaced works by Poussin.

The gilt-bronze clock made for Louis XV, the two Sèvres porcelain vases placed here under Louis XVI along with the busts of Alexander and Scipio, are all fine examples of the furnishings which filled this room under the *Ancien Régime*. The draped table and folding stools denote the purpose of this room where, for centuries, some of France's most important historical decisions were taken.

▲
THE COUNCIL
CHAMBER

CENTER : THE CLOCK CABINET ▶
RIGHT : THE BEDCHAMBER ▶

The King's Private Apartment

The King's Private Apartment lies beyond the mirrored-door separating the Council Chamber from Louis XV's Bedchamber. Formerly this suite was a series of drawing rooms where Louis XIV had set up some of the finest pieces of his collections, as well as certain rooms for his personal leisure such as a billiards room. Apprehensive of the lack of comfort in his ancestor's bedchamber, Louis XV decided in 1738 to have a real apartment designed for himself. Following the logical order of things, it was entered via a guardroom on the ground floor, then reached from the *Degré du Roi* or King's Staircase ; the latter, built in 1754, was extended to reach the second storey in 1763.

The *Cabinet des Chiens* (Cabinet of the Dogs), a sort of antechamber to this apartment, was decorated with woodwork from Louis XIV's billiards room (converted into a bedchamber for Louis XV). It leads into a room used for several purposes under Louis XV before becoming the after-hunt dining room, itself connected to the King's Private Cabinets. It also leads into a large room decorated with woodwork by Verberckt, and which was known as the Oval, or Clock, drawing room in 1738. After 1760 this room became known as the *Cabinet de la Pendule* or Clock Cabinet when it was remodelled to appear as it does today. This is when the famous astronomical clock, the work of Passemant who had ordered the sculpted case himself from the Caffieris, was placed here.

The Clock Cabinet was used as a games room by Louis XV ; however, following the traditional layout of apartments, it was an antechamber to the actual bedchamber as well as the *Cabinet de Travail*, or Work Cabinet (also known as the *Cabinet Intérieur*, or Private Cabinet) in contrast with the State Cabinet, or Council Chamber.

The bedchamber was the room where the king actually slept, whereas the large bedchamber made for Louis XIV was only used for etiquette. The woodwork was extensively changed several times, and aside from the gold brocade silk lining the alcove — a replica of the original woven in 1785 for Louis XVI's summer furnishings — the original furniture has not been restored. The celadon fountain mounted with gilt-bronze which now stands on the mantelpiece was originally part of the furnishings of the *Garde Robe*, or dressing room, next door under Louis XV.

The dressing room, alte-
ed for Louis XVI in 1788,
was the last room to be
designed for the king
before the Revolution.

Louis XV died here on
May 10, 1774. He had
been very fond of history,
and had ordered portraits
to be placed above the
doors, including "Fran-
çois I" by Titian. Those
works are now replaced
by portraits of his daugh-
ers, after Nattier.

On the other side of the
Clock Cabinet lies the
King's Private Cabinet
and an annex or *arrière-
cabinet*. It was in here that
both Louis XV and Louis
XVI worked. The Private
Cabinet was altered seve-
al times, from 1738 when
it became the *"cabinet à
pans"* (due to its cut-off
corners), to 1760 when it
was changed to appear as
it does today. This room is
one of the most faithfully
redecorated in the entire
château, as the furniture is
all authentic, dating from
1769 to 1780. It includes
such fine pieces as the
famous desk of the king
(Riesener), the medal ca-
binet (Gaudreaux) and the
corner cupboards (Jou-
bert). The Sèvres porce-
lain vases and the famous
candelabra commemora-
ting American Indepen-
dence atop the medal
cabinet were all created at
a later date, but specifically for this room under
Louis XVI.

The New Rooms

The *Salles Neuves*,
(New Rooms), a late
extension to the King's
Private Apartment, in-
cluded the *Cabinet de la
Vaisselle d'or"* (Gold Plate
Cabinet), a library, a
dining room known as the
Porcelain Room, a bil-

THE KING'S
PRIVATE CABINET

LOUIS XVI'S
LIBRARY

OVERLEAF : THE PORCELAIN DINING ROOM ▶
BELOW : THE ROYAL HUNT ▶

47

liards room and a Game
Room.

Originally Madame d
Montespan's Apartmen
these rooms were replace
by the *Petite Galerie* an
the two drawing room
decorated by Mignard i
1684. This suite was rea
ched via the Ambassador
Staircase, and designed t
house some of the king
paintings. The *Petit
Galerie* was replaced i
1752 by an apartment fo
Madame Adélaide, Loui
XV's eldest daughter
which included Loui
XIV's former Medal Ca

THE SIEGE OF FREIBUR
THE GAMES ROO

binet. Louis XV took over the rooms in 1769, but their present décor is more reminiscent of Louis XVI ; the small medal cabinet and porcelain plates in the first room, (leading into Louis XV's formerly bath-chamber later the *"Très Arrière Cabinet"* by his grandson) ; tables by Riesener and painted pekin curtains in the Library, created upon Louis XVI's succession by Gabriel, whose last work it was to be ; sky blue curtains, simple chairs with mouldings and porcelain plates in the Dining Room, which originally had white wainscoting ; brocade-covered chairs, corner cupboards and, finally, gouaches by Van Blarenberghe depicting Louis XV's battles in the Games Room.

THE KING'S PRIVATE CABINETS

When standing outside the château it is difficult to imagine that there lies, above the King's Private Apartment, a suite of rooms spread out over several floors which were the private domain of Louis XV and Louis XVI. Their purpose, as well as their décor, changed several times according to either the king's needs or fancy. These include the Library and its annexes; the Geography and Physics Cabinets, which bear witness to the interests of Louis XV as well as Louis XVI's taste for study and research; the dining rooms, Games Room and *Petite Galerie*, replaced by apartments which the King had made for those privileged enough to share his privacy. These rooms all point to the ruler's romantic or friendly attachments and, in spite of subsequent alterations, certain apartments still bear the names of those for whom these special rooms were created, such as Madame du Barry's room offered by Louis XV to his *"favorite"*, and the minister Maurepas who had won the favor of Louis XVI. Despite restoration efforts, the present state of these rooms, with their fine woodwork, are only a pale reminder of the refined décor they once knew.

▲ THE KING'S STAIRCASE
◀ MADAME DU BARRY'S APARTMENT

THE GROUND FLOOR OF
THE MAIN BUILDING

It has been with a constant wish for authenticity that the ground floor of the main building has been restored — and often reconstructed — in order to capture the 18th century flavor it had when the Dauphin, the Dauphine, and Mesdames the daughters of Louis XV lived in this section of the château. The original wainscoting has been replaced in some places, copied in others or reproduced thanks to mouldings. The *Galerie Basse*, or Lower Gallery, linking the Dauphin's Apartment to Madame Victoire's, was recreated based on the previous design and a careful study of 18th-century plans and archives.

These princely apartments unfortunately contain few of the original furnishings, but the history of 18th-century France is recalled here thanks to Louis-Philippe.

GROUND FLOOR OF THE CHATEAU

THE DAUPHINE'S APARTMENT
1. 1st Antechamber (42)
2. 2nd Antechamber (43)
3. State Cabinet (44)
4. Bedchamber (45)
5. Private Cabinet (46)
6. *Arrières Cabinets* of the duchesse d'Angoulême

THE DAUPHIN'S APARTMENT
7. Library (47)
8. State Cabinet (48)
9. Bedchamber (49)
10. *Arrières Cabinets*
11. 2nd Antechamber (50)

12. *GALERIE BASSE* (51) (Lower Gallery)

MADAME VICTOIRE'S APARTMENT
13. 1st Antechamber (52)
14. *Salon des Nobles* (53)
15. State Cabinet (54)
16. Bedchamber (55)
17. Private Cabinet (56 a)
18. Library (56 b)

AILE DU MIDI (SOUTH WING)

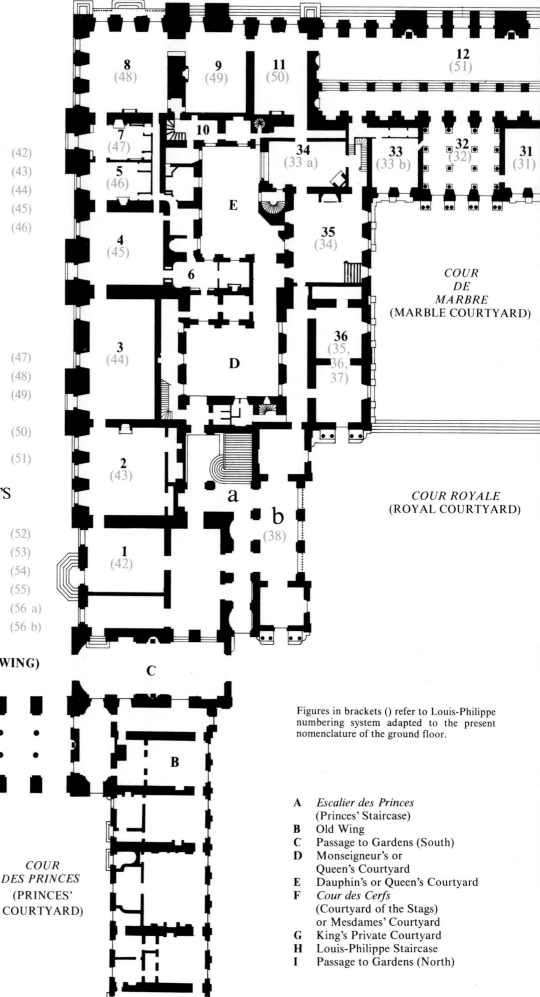

COUR DE MARBRE (MARBLE COURTYARD)

COUR ROYALE (ROYAL COURTYARD)

Figures in brackets () refer to Louis-Philippe numbering system adapted to the present nomenclature of the ground floor.

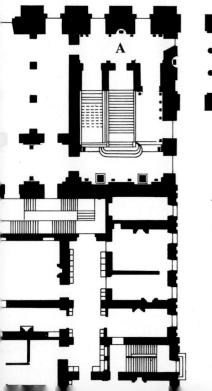

COUR DES PRINCES (PRINCES' COURTYARD)

A   *Escalier des Princes* (Princes' Staircase)
B   Old Wing
C   Passage to Gardens (South)
D   Monseigneur's or Queen's Courtyard
E   Dauphin's or Queen's Courtyard
F   *Cour des Cerfs* (Courtyard of the Stags) or Mesdames' Courtyard
G   King's Private Courtyard
H   Louis-Philippe Staircase
I   Passage to Gardens (North)

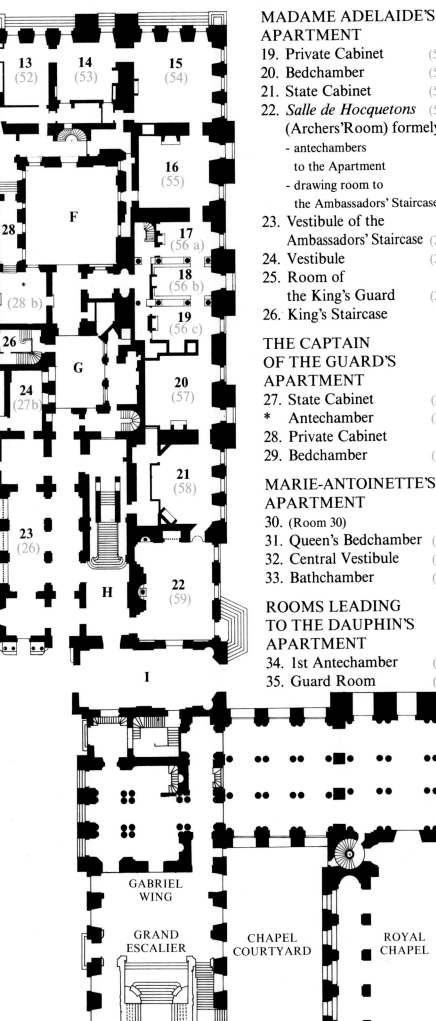

MADAME ADELAIDE'S APARTMENT
19. Private Cabinet (56 c)
20. Bedchamber (57)
21. State Cabinet (58)
22. *Salle de Hocquetons* (59) (Archers' Room) formely :
    - antechambers to the Apartment
    - drawing room to the Ambassadors' Staircase
23. Vestibule of the Ambassadors' Staircase (26)
24. Vestibule (27 b)
25. Room of the King's Guard (27 a)
26. King's Staircase

THE CAPTAIN OF THE GUARD'S APARTMENT
27. State Cabinet (28 a)
* Antechamber (28 b)
28. Private Cabinet
29. Bedchamber (29)

MARIE-ANTOINETTE'S APARTMENT
30. (Room 30)
31. Queen's Bedchamber (31)
32. Central Vestibule (32)
33. Bathchamber (33 b)

ROOMS LEADING TO THE DAUPHIN'S APARTMENT
34. 1st Antechamber (33 a)
35. Guard Room (34)

THE KING'S *GARDE-ROBE* (Dressing Room)
36. (Rooms 35, 36, 37)

a. THE QUEEN'S STAIRCASE

b. Vestibule (38)

LOUIS XIV'S BATHCHAMBER
(52) *Bath Cabinet*
(53) *Bath Chamber*
(54) *Formerly the Salon Octogone*
(55) Ionic Room or Formerly the Doric
(56) Vestibule (later divided up into 56 a, b and c)

The various redistributions of rooms throughout the centuries have led to numerous changes in this part of the château. The purpose of this floorplan is to illustrate most of the detailed configurations to come out of recent restoration work. Visitors are also informed that in spite of the fact that the tour suggested in these pages follows the logical layout of the suites (e.g. the Apartments of the Dauphine or Madame Victoire), the tour is often conducted "backwards" for practical reasons (e.g. the Apartments of the Dauphin or Madame Adelaide).

AILE DU NORD (NORTH WING)

several times. They were originally the apartments of Louis XIV's brother, the duc d'Orléans, and his wife the Princess Palatine; the Grand Dauphin, son of the Sun King, lived here next. While Louis XV was still a minor, the Regent took over the rooms, and it was for the son of the former and his second wife Marie-Josèphe de Saxe that this part of the château was decorated in the style adopted by 20th-century curators. This includes the Dauphine's State Cabinet with its console, a reminder of the fine woodwork which once adorned the room; her Private Cabinet, extensively restored, and the library and bedchamber of the Dauphin, fortunately preserved.

These apartments were once again transformed at the end of the reign of Louis XV for the Dauphine Marie-Antoinette and the future Louis XVI, under whom the comte and comtesse de Provence, then the Children of France, lived here. These changes continued until the *Restauration* (including the private cabinets of the duchesse d'Angoulême) before Louis Philippe had the rooms transformed into the Admirals' Room and the first Marshals' Rooms.

Nowadays, aside from the restoration of the former apartments, it is the Regency and the first part of Louis XV's reign which are depicted here, including an extraordinary collection of portraits of the Princesses of the Royal Family by Nattier.

After crossing the Lower Gallery visitors enter the apartments of Madame Victoire and her sister Madame Adélaide.

Some of the finest portraits by Nattier, Van Loo and Vigée-Lebrun conserved by the château can be seen in these rooms.

Visitors should bear in mind that this part of the château has only been partially reconstituted, explaining the considerable discrepancy in luxuriousness between the various suites. The apartments of the Children of France face the gardens and, like the first storey, the tour of these rooms does not necessarily follow the logical layout of the suite.

The Dauphine's Apartment takes up the first five rooms. The Dauphin's Apartment follows, and its four rooms should really be toured starting from the Guard Room facing the Marble Courtyard, and the first antechamber. Since the initial construction of Versailles, these two suites have been altered

▲
THE DAUPHINE'S
PRIVATE CABINET

They lived here, in these rather dreary rooms facing the North Parterre, until the Revolution. This was the site of the sumptuous bath apartment in Louis XIV's time which was little by little altered and destroyed to make room for the apartments of Madame de Montespan, the comtesse de Toulouse, Madame de Pompadour and finally Mesdames, daughters of Louis XV. The only trace of the bath apartment are the columns in the vestibule which were enclosed when this section was separated into private cabinets and libraries for

▲
THE DAUPHIN'S GRAND CABINET

THE DAUPHIN'S BEDCHAMBER ▶

he daughters of the *Bien-Aimé*. Louis-Philippe had them uncovered when he had the Marshals' rooms designed in this part of the château ; the columns were then hidden away once again by wood paneling (or, at any rate, replicas of the originals) for Madame Adélaide's Private Cabinet. (This apartment is visited in the opposite direction of the logical layout of the rooms).

The hangings in the rooms of the two princesses are replicas of the 1769-89 summer furnishings.

▲
MADAME ADELAIDE (NATTIER)

FETE GIVEN BY THE PRINCE DE CONTI, BY OLLIVIER ▶

The Museum of the History of France portrays the Royal Family and social life in the late 1700s with, in particular, Olliviers's paintings of the prince de Conti in Madame Victoire's first antechamber. The two corner cupboards made by Péridrez were commissioned by Joubert for the bedchamber.

The rooms facing the Marble Courtyard (with the exception of Marie Antoinette's small bedchamber and bathchamber along the central vestibule) evoke the end

MADAME VICTOIRE'S
◀ BEDCHAMBER

MADAME VICTOIRE'S
GRAND CABINET   MADAME ADELAIDE'S
GRAND CABINET

Louis XV's reign and that of Louis XVI. Under the *Ancien Régime* these rooms were plainly furnished in contrast with those looking out onto the gardens, and include : the Guard Room and foot of the King's Staircase where, in 1757, Damiens attempted to assassinate Louis XV ; the apartment of the Captain of the Guards which features several famous works hung on red velvet, such as the portrait of Marie-Antoinette holding a rose by Mme Vigée-Lebrun, and the two paintings by Hubert Robert depicting the replantation of the gardens in 1775. The Dauphin's Guard Room on the other side of the Marble Courtyard completes the reign of Louis XVI. The neighboring rooms, formerly the King's dressing rooms, feature valuable pastels.

PORTRAIT OF MARIE-ANTOINETTE HOLDING A ROSE,
BY MADAME VIGEE-LEBRUN

59

The Consulate and Empire Rooms

There is no doubt that Versailles was the first museum of Napoleonic history, and the entire ground floor of the south wing commemorates the Empire in a fine example of 19th-century museology, part of Louis-Philippe's project to unite France's various *régimes*. Following the museum's reorganization at the turn of the century, the rooms on the second storey above the Queen's Apartment (know as the Chimay Attic), as well as those along the ceiling of the Hall of Battles, are also devoted to the Consulate and Empire. Works relating to the French Revolution have recently been added to this collection ; they were formerly exhibited on the ground floor, following Louis XVI's reign. These rooms are reached via an extension of the Queen's Staircase.

Apart from masterpieces by David and Gros, sketches by Gérard, drawings by Dutertre, paintings by Lejeune and gouaches by Bagetti are exhibited here and provide a colorful and vivid rendering of life in Napoleon's time.

The North wing and 19th-Century Rooms

The second storey of the north wing commemorates the events and depicts the figures who made history under France's various governments after the fall of Napoleon in 1815. The *Restauration* is presented first with the two kings Louis XVIII and Charles X, whose importance is too often minimized. After the revolution of 1830 their cousin Louis-Philippe d'Orléans came to the throne ; it was thanks to his personal fortune that Versailles was saved when he transformed the château into a museum. After the revolution of 1848 and the Second Republic, France was ruled by Napoleon III under the Second Empire which lasted until the war of 1870-1871. The defeat in 1871 led to the Third Republic and French retaliation during World War I (1914-1918), which ended in the Treaty of Versailles signed here in the Hall of Mirrors.

This completes the Museum of the History of France. Gérard, Gros, Horace Vernet and Winterhalter are some of the distinguished artists whose works are displayed here.

More large rooms dealing with the 19th century are presently being restored. They look out onto the stone gallery on the first storey of the north wing, and will feature such major works as the capture of the Smalah of AbdelKader by Horace Vernet, and the coronation of Charles X by Gérard.

▲
ABOVE : THE CAIRO UPRISING, BY GIRODET
◄ LEFT : NAPOLEON'S ENTRY OF BERLIN, BY MEYNIER

▲
LOUIS-PHILIPPE
AND HIS SONS, BY H. VERNET

The Royal Opera

Vocal music was an essential part of entertainment at Versailles, and as early as 1685 Hardouin-Mansart had planned the construction of an opera room at the tip of the north wing. This project was never carried through, nor was Gabriel's initial design for an opera to be built on the same spot. But the plan was not abandoned and, in 1769, Gabriel was commissioned to build a theater in anticipation of the festivities and entertainment held in honor of the mariage of the Dauphin (Louis XVI) to the Archduchess of Austria-Lorraine, Marie-Antoinette. The magnificent opera, with its harmonious tones of blue, pink and gold, was built for this occasion.

It has an elliptical shape and is made up of a dress circle and two floors of boxes above the parterre with, in the middle, the Royal Box. A row of ionic order columns forms a second balcony divided into boxes ; a third level could be created between the two permanent ones if required. Though this room was specifically created as an opera room, it could also be used for fancy dress balls, when a backdrop mirroring the layout of the balconies and boxes was temporarily set up on the stage.

The ceiling painting is the work of Durameau and depicts the triumph of Apollo ; it was mounted here once again during restoration work in 1957. The opera had been painted in red and gold under Louis-Philippe for the wedding of the royal prince, and was considerably damaged while the Senate sat here under the Third Republic. The vast curtain, featuring the arms of France embroidered in gold on sky blue silk, was also restored in the 1950.

The foyer, at one time preceded by a guard room (taken down under Napoleon III to make room for the Questel staircase), is an essential complement to the actual theater ; it is decorated with trompe-l'œil paintings and sculptures by Pajou, with wood and stucco imitations of stone, bronze and marble.

THE ROYAL OPERA ▶

THE GARDENS AND GROVES

"On leaving the château by the vestibule opening onto the Marble Courtyard, one reaches the terrace ; one should pause at the top of the steps to take in the layout of the parterres, ponds and fountains as seen from the Cabinets. One should then continue straight ahead to the top of the Latona parterre, and pause there to look at Latona, the lizards, the ramps, the statues, the Royal Avenue, the Fountain of Apollo and the canal, and then look back at the parterre and the château."

This advice, given by Louis XIV himself in his "Manner of presenting the gardens Versailles", is without a doubt the best guidebook available, as the gardens at Versailles have as much, if not more, importance than the château itself. Le Nôtre, when drawing the plans for the gardens, (and despite changes made at a later date), retained the large axes laid out under Louis XIII. However, following the king's precise wishes, he broadened the vistas, increased the number of ponds, created the groves, and gathered a fine collection of 17th-century statues.

VIEW OF THE GARDENS CIRCA 1700,
◄ BY J.B. MARTIN (DETAIL)

THE SOUTH PARTERRE
IN SUMMER

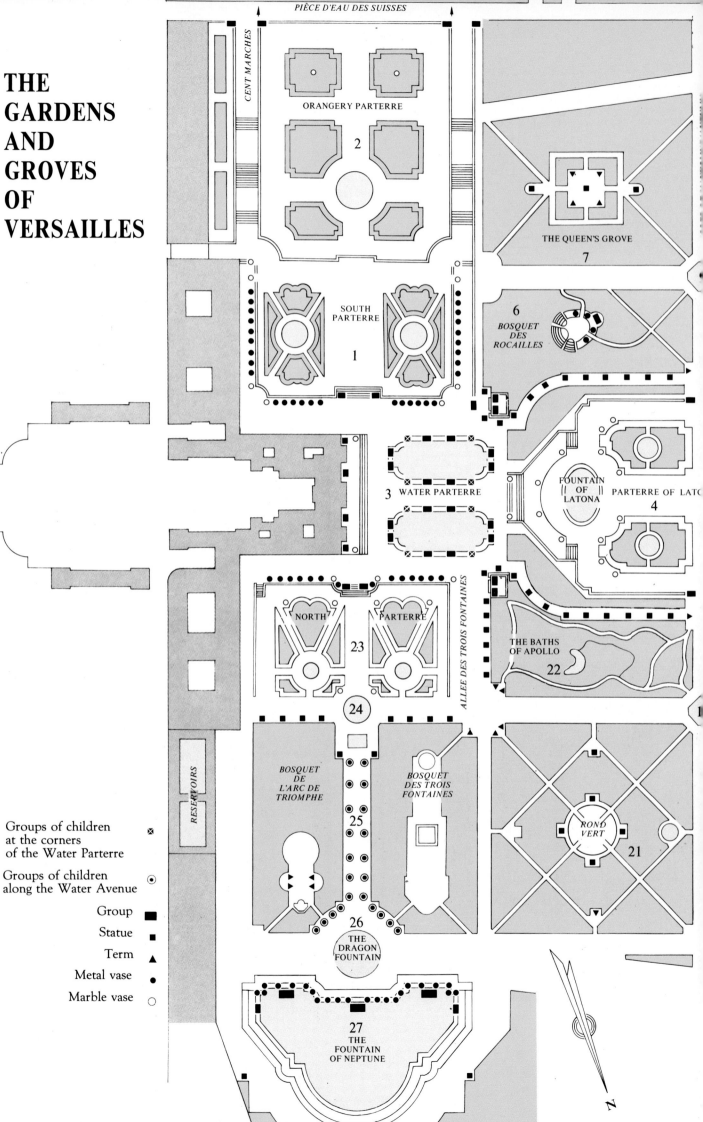

THE GARDENS AND GROVES OF VERSAILLES

PIÈCE D'EAU DES SUISSES

CENT MARCHES

ORANGERY PARTERRE

2

THE QUEEN'S GROVE

7

SOUTH PARTERRE

1

6

BOSQUET DES ROCAILLES

3 WATER PARTERRE

FOUNTAIN OF LATONA

PARTERRE OF LATO...

4

NORTH PARTERRE

23

THE BATHS OF APOLLO

22

ALLÉE DES TROIS FONTAINES

24

RESERVOIRS

BOSQUET DE L'ARC DE TRIOMPHE

BOSQUET DES TROIS FONTAINES

25

ROND VERT

21

Groups of children at the corners of the Water Parterre ⊠

Groups of children along the Water Avenue ⊙

Group ■

Statue ▪

Term ▲

Metal vase ●

Marble vase ○

26

THE DRAGON FOUNTAIN

27

THE FOUNTAIN OF NEPTUNE

N

66

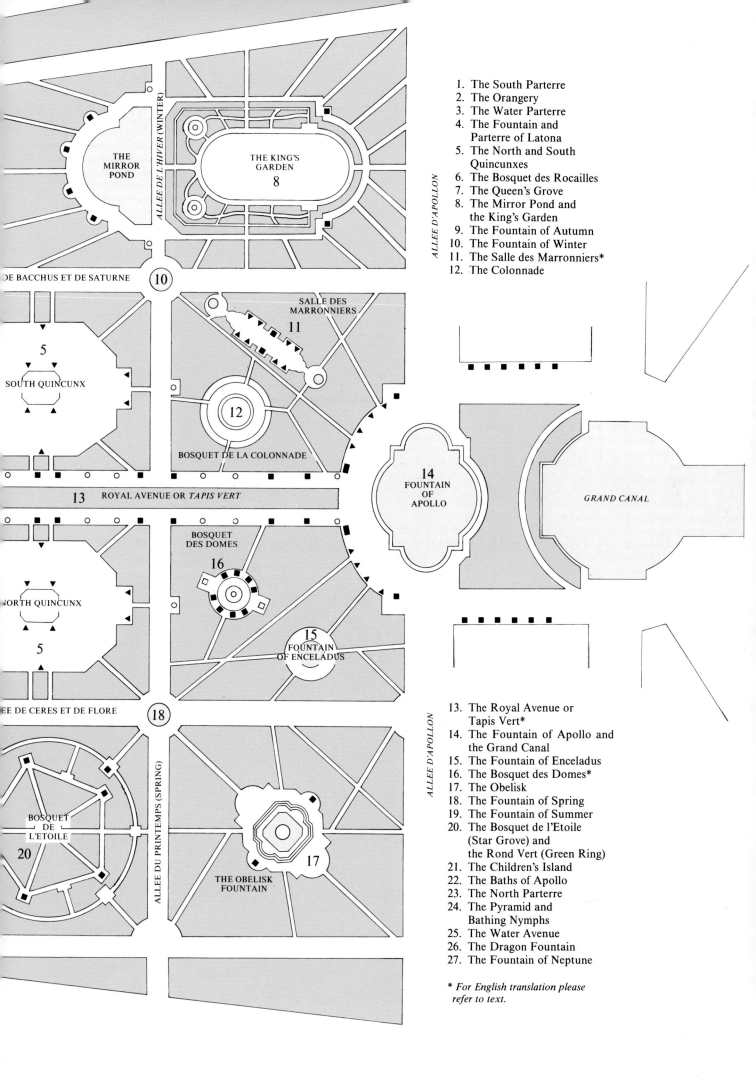

1. The South Parterre
2. The Orangery
3. The Water Parterre
4. The Fountain and Parterre of Latona
5. The North and South Quincuxes
6. The Bosquet des Rocailles
7. The Queen's Grove
8. The Mirror Pond and the King's Garden
9. The Fountain of Autumn
10. The Fountain of Winter
11. The Salle des Marronniers*
12. The Colonnade

13. The Royal Avenue or Tapis Vert*
14. The Fountain of Apollo and the Grand Canal
15. The Fountain of Enceladus
16. The Bosquet des Domes*
17. The Obelisk
18. The Fountain of Spring
19. The Fountain of Summer
20. The Bosquet de l'Etoile (Star Grove) and the Rond Vert (Green Ring)
21. The Children's Island
22. The Baths of Apollo
23. The North Parterre
24. The Pyramid and Bathing Nymphs
25. The Water Avenue
26. The Dragon Fountain
27. The Fountain of Neptune

*For English translation please refer to text.

67

The South Parterre

The South Parterre, with its intricately-designed flower beds, is lined with bronze vases atop slabs of marble ; it is supported by the roof of the Orangery, visible from the staircase flanked by statues of children on a sphinx (Lerambert and Sarrazin). The design of the parterre, which provides a view of the *Pièce d'eau des Suisses* (lake of the Swiss Guards) and the statue of Louis XIV (Bernini), was in fact modified several times ; from 1687 to 1701 bronze statues (replicas of ancient works had stood here but are now placed against the west façade of the main building. The two ramps known as the *Cent Marches* (Hundred Steps), flanking the Orangery to the east and west, can be seen from the balustrade looking south.

▲
THE SOUTH PARTERRE
BRONZE VASE

THE ORANGERY PARTERRE AND THE WEST
RAMP OF THE CENT MARCHES ▶

The Orangery

The Orangery was built by Hardouin-Mansart from 1684 to 1686 and replaced the former orangery built by Le Vau. This vast edifice, the presence of which cannot be guessed when looking from the South Parterre (which it supports), is made up of three galleries encircling a parterre. In summer 1200 palm trees, pomegranates and orange trees are brought out and placed along the paths. The central gallery, 508 feet long, 42 feet wide and 43 feet high, features a statue of Louis XIV by Desjardins. The lateral galleries extend below the ramps and are 350 feet long.

The Orangery, unique in its majestic proportions, maintains a steady temperature never dropping below 6°C (42,8°F) in both winter and summer. Under the *Ancien Régime* 2000 orange trees, 1000 oleander and pomegranates were kept here, and palm trees were added in the 19th century.

CENTRAL VIEW
◀ OF THE ORANGERY

The Water Parterre

Still following Louis XIV's description of Versailles, visitors reach the *Parterre d'Eau* (Water Parterre) by going down the steps of the terrace flanking the main building and decorated with two marble sculptures, the War Vase by Coysevox and the Peace Vase by Tubi. This parterre owes its name to the two large rectangular ponds ; after several changes it took on its final appearance when the bronze statues by the Kellers were created between 1683 and 1690. Cast after sculptures by the greatest artists of the time — Coysevox, Tubi, Le Hongre and Regnaudin — they represent the main rivers and streams of France. These figures complement the glory of the French kingdom depicted by the famous classical groups representing the Nile and the Tibrus. The sculptures of the Water Parterre, along with the Peace and War vases, the ceiling paintings in the Hall of Mirrors, the War drawing room and the Peace drawing room, express with triumph the convictions of those for whom the reign of the Sun King measured up to that of the ancient Roman emperor Augustus.

▲
THE WATER
PARTERRE

THE FOUNTAIN OF LATONA AND
THE EAST-WEST AXIS ▶

The Fountain of Latona and Parterre

The Fountain of Latona is situated below the Water Parterre and is named after Latona, mother of Diana and Apollo. Having been scoffed at by the peasants of Lycia, she was revenged when Jupiter, the father of her children, turned the accused into frogs.

This pond already existed under Louis XIII, but was only completed in 1670 when the central fountain by Marsy was built. Originally facing the château, the Latona group now faces west, perhaps owing to the alterations carried out when Hardouin-Mansart built the three levels depicting the metamorphisis of the Lycians.

In the middle of the two parterres on either side of the Fountain of Latona are two ponds each with a fountain also depicting

the metamorphisis of the Lycians.

The Fountain of Latona is reached either by the central staircase or the two ramps on either side flanked by classical statues, most of which are copies of ancient works. Fifteen of the eighteen statues were executed after sketches by Lebrun.

The East-West Axis

The *Tapis Vert* (Green Carpet) stretches west from the Latona Parterre on a gentle slope. It is lined with statues and vases and is the central alley of the garden's main axis ; the lawn and paths are 1100 feet long and 210 feet wide.

The bosquets, or groves, lie to the north and south, hidden by the foliage. The romantic flavor of this part of the gardens only dates from 1774-1777 when, under the guidance of Hubert Robert, Louis XVI had the gardens replanted. Despite alterations, most of the groves can be traced back to designs by Le Nôtre.

The North and South Quincunxes

The symmetrical North and South Quincunxes are decorated with marble terms made in Rome (after works by Poussin) commissioned by Fouquet and bought from the latter by Louis XIV.

The South Quincunxes have replaced the *Bosquet de la Girandole* (Candelabra grove), and the North Quincunxes the Dauphin Grove.

NORTH QUINCUNX
FAUN (AFTER POUSSIN) ▶

Le Bosquet des Rocailles (Rockwork Grove)

This grove was created between 1681 and 1683 and is probably one of the most spectacular in the gardens of Versailles. It was known as "the ballroom" because of the marble floor which once took up the center of the grove. Guests who did not partake in the dancing sat on the tiers near the entrance. The other semicircle is decorated with rockwork cascades above which rise gilt-lead vases by Leconte and Le Hongre, marking the spot where the musicians stood. The large candlestands by Le Gros, Mazeline and Jouvenet were designed to hold candelabra.

THE BOSQUET
DES ROCAILLES ▶

The Mirror Pond and the King's Garden

The Mirror Pond, shaped like a farthingale, was built in 1672, and was later part of a garden surrounded by fences, trees, statues and vases completed in 1674-1683 along with the Royal Island. This area had become a swamp by the 19th century and had been abandoned ; Louis XVIII, when commissioning his architect Dufour to restore Versailles, had a garden with lawns, flower shrubs and winding paths built here which became known as the King's Garden.

La Salle des Marronniers (Hall of Chestnut Trees)

This grove, at one time called the Hall of Classical Statues then the Water Gallery, was originally lined with yew trees and decorated with ponds and statues. This long alley near the *Colonnade* was entirely redesigned in 1704-06, and numerous classical busts (authentic or replicas) were placed here at that time.

The Queen's Grove

The Queen's Grove was one of several created in 1774-75 when Hubert Robert replanted the gardens. These English-style groves contrasted with the bosquets designed by Le Nôtre, as well as his labyrinth, created on this site in 1673. A few lead sculptures originally painted in natural tones remain from the labyrinth, which had no less than 39 fountains each representing a theme from Aesop's fables. The sculptures are now preserved in the Musée de l'Oeuvre housed in the north and northeastern galleries of the *Grande Ecurie* (still under construction).

ABOVE : THE MIRROR POND ▲
AND THE KING'S GARDEN

RIGHT : THE QUEEN'S GROVE ▶

The Fountains of Autumn and Winter

Four fountains mark the cross-roads formed by the main avenues of the gardens on either side of the *Tapis Vert*. Their construction began in 1672 following plans by Lebrun, and they each represent one of the four seasons and the gods symbolizing them.

Curiously enough the cold seasons lie south of the central alley :

— Autumn, represented by Bacchus, is the work of Marsy (1673-1675) and shaped in an octagon.

— Winter, depicted by Saturn, was executed by Girardon (1675-1677) and is circular in shape.

An unsucessful attempt was made a few years ago to recreate the 17th century polychrome décor of the fountains.

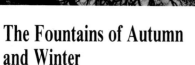

▲
THE FOUNTAIN OF WINTER

THE FOUNTAIN OF AUTUMN ▶

74

The Colonnade

This spot is unique in the gardens of Versailles due to its imposing architectural design, the fruit of close collaboration between Hardouin-Mansart and Le Nôtre. The Colonnade, which replaced the *Parterre des Sources* in 1685, is a circular peristyle of 32 Ionic-order columns made of various types of marble. The columns, coupled with Languedoc marble pilasters, support arches crowned each with a white marble cornice and 32 urns in line with the columns. The tympani are decorated with reliefs depicting cupids playing music, evoking the fact that this grove was long used for concerts. Under each arch lies a wide basin equipped with a fountain.

The great artists who took part in the decoration of this magnificent piece of architecture were Coysevox, Tubi, Le Hongre, Le Conte, Mazière and Granier. A pedestal lies in the center of the area, marking the spot where the sculpted group by Girardon depicting the Rape of Persephone (1699) once

stood ; it has now been housed in the Musée de l'Oeuvre to protect it from bad weather, and will be replaced by a copy.

The *Tapis Vert*

The Royal Avenue is also known as the *Tapis Vert* (Green Carpet), because of the vast lawn which runs down the center of the strip. 1100 feet long and 210 feet wide, the Alley is lined with twelve statues and twelve vases, and features the two large ponds dedicated to Apollo. The birth of the deity representing the new day is illustrated by both the Fountain of Latona and the course of the sun symbolized by Apollo on his chariot.

▲
THE COLONNADE

◀ THE TAPIS VERT

75

The Fountain of Apollo and the Grand Canal

At the bottom of the *Tapis Vert* lies a halfmoon adorned with twelve statues and terms, the majority of which are 17th-century copies of ancient classical works. The original pond, dug here in 1639 under Louis XIII, became known as the Pond of the Swans after alterations under Louis XIV. It was in 1671 that Tubi created the magnificent lead sculpture from sketches by Lebrun after l'Albane. Here the God of the Sun and the Arts is depicted emerging from the water on a chariot drawn by four horses surrounded by dolphins and tritons. As if to contradict Nature, but flatter the Sun King, Apollo emerges from the West and heads towards the East, where lies Versailles and the home of Louis XIV.

Beyond lies the Grand Canal, 5118 feet long and 394 feet wide, intersected a third of the way down by a branch 3376 feet in length which stretches south towards the site of the former *Ménagerie* north of the Trianon, seemingly perpetuating the perspective of the main axis to the West and an endless horizon.

The canal was begun in 1667-1668 and completed in 1680. As early as 1669 great "naval" festivities were held here, and in 1687 several Venetian gondoliers were put in charge of the flotilla which sailed this stretch of water, and lived in the small buildings north of the Fountain of Apollo ; the site is still known as Little Venice.

THE FOUNTAIN
OF APOLLO ▶

The Fountain of Enceladus

According to legend Enceladus was one of the giants who had attempted to scale Mount Olympus and dethrone Jupiter, who defeated them and buried them in a mass of rocks.

Marsy executed this figure in 1676 in the center of the pond now bearing the giant's name. The fallen Titan, portrayed by the sculptor with extraordinary pathos, struggles amidst the rocks in a final effort. An 85 feet high jet springs from the giant's mouth when the fountains are in play.

THE FOUNTAIN
OF ENCELADUS

THE BOSQUET
DES DOMES ▶

The *Bosquet des Dômes*

When walking back towards the château on a path facing north of the Royal Alley, visitors come across several groves which, though differing from those lying south, were designed to achieve symmetry with them.

The *Bosquet des Dômes* (Grove of the Domes) was probably altered more than all the others, as early as the 17th century.

In 1677-78, Hardouin-Mansart had built two pavilions facing one another, whose foundations still exist ; remains of the buildings are now kept in the Musée de l'Oeuvre. A statue of Fame stood in the center of the octogonal pond until 1684, and for a time the bosquet was known by this name. Then, in 1686, sculptures which had been made for the Grotto of Tethys were placed between the pavilions (the grotto had been taken down when the north wing was built).

Among these statues the famous group of Apollo and his horses stood here until 1704. However, most of the statues removed under Louis-Philippe have been put back on the pedestals specially designed for them by Caffieri.

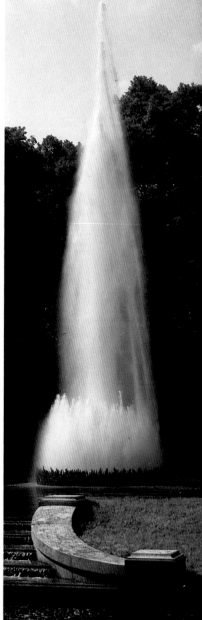

The Obelisk Fountain

This fountain was only built in 1706 and is the work of Hardouin-Mansart. It replaced the *Salle du Conseil* (Council Chamber) also known as the *Salle des Festins* (Banquet Hall). The pond is built up above the ground surrounding it ; its center is decorated with a clump of reeds from which some 230 jets of water spring to form an aquatic pyramid, rising as high as 85 feet.

▲
THE OBELISK
FOUNTAIN

79

The Fountains of Spring and Summer

The Fountains of Spring and Summer, parallel to the Fountains of Autumn and Winter, are dedicated to Flora and Ceres.

Flora, seated before a bed of flowers in a circular pond, is the work of Tubi (1672-75).

Cérès, in an octagonal pond, was executed by Regnaudin (1672-74).

Like the two other fountains dedicated to the Seasons, the Fountains of Spring and Summer were executed after sketches by Lebrun.

Unsuccessful attempts at recreated the original polychrome gilding have recently been carried out.

◄ THE FOUNTAIN
OF SUMMER

▲
THE CHILDREN'S ISLAND
THE FOUNTAIN OF SPRING ▶

The Children's Island

This charming group known as the *Ile des Enfants*, or Children's Island, depicts children playing on a rock while two cupids splash about in the water. The sculpted group is the work of Hardy ; it originally stood in the gardens of the first Trianon, the Porcelain Trianon, and was moved here in 1710.

Walking eastwards one comes across a simple lawn-covered dip. It is difficult to imagine that on this spot Le Nôtre had succeeded in creating one of his most ingenious hydraulic works, the Water Theater.

The *Bosquet de l'Etoile*, (Star Grove), near the North Quincunx, is made up of a simple circle with five paths radiating towards another circular path. It replaced the so-called Water Mountain in 1704 when the somewhat baroque forms of amusement were becoming less fashionable, and the trend was towards greater moderation ; fifty years later English-style gardens and "quaint" constructions were to become the rule.

The Baths of Apollo

The design of this grove, the work of Hubert Robert (1778),comes as a surprise in contrast with the general harmony prevailing in the gardens at Versailles. It was created to shelter the sculptures by Girardon and Regnaudin of Apollo being tended by Nymphs and the Sun Horses by Marsy and Régnaudin. They had originally been intended for the Grotto of Thetys, but were moved to the Grove of the Domes before being set up here in 1704 under a canopy. They stand on the site of the former *Bassin du Marais* (Swamp Pond) supposedly the idea of Madame de Montespan, the King's declared mistress. This sculpture of Apollo's bath, presented as it was under Louis XVI, seems unapproachable, and the mysterious flavor of the artifical grotto sheltering the group does not alter the disappointment one feels at not being able to admire more closely these masterpieces of French statuary.

THE BATHS
OF APOLLO ▶

82

The North Parterre

"One shall then move on to the Pyramid, and pause for a moment. Then one shall approach the château once again by way of the marble staircase between the Knifegrinder and the kneeling Venus, turn around at the top of the steps to take in the North Parterre, the statues, vases, crowns, the Pyramid, and what can be seen of Neptune. One shall then leave the garden through the same door one used to enter it." Thus Louis XIV himself com-

▲
THE NORTH PARTERRE

▲
THE PYRAMID FOUNTAIN

84

pletes the tour of the gardens of Versailles, with the northern part of the North-South axis.

In contrast with the South Parterre ending in a terrace supported by the Orangery, beyond which the *Pièce d'Eau des Suisses* blends into an endless horizon, the North Parterre is made up of large triangular lawns and paths. Its perspective is impaired by the Pyramid Fountain by Girardon (1669-70) after Lebrun. Further on, the extraordinary fountain of the Bathing Nymphs, a bas-relief of reserved sensuality, is the work of Girardon, here demonstrating his exceptional talent.

The *Water Avenue*

In order to admire the fountain of the Bathing Nymphs, one must approach the group from the north after walking up an avenue lined with fountains held up by children, the *Allée d'Eau* (Water Avenue), or *Allée des Marmousets* (Small Children).

These original founains, lining the gentle slope beyond the Pyramid Fountain, were apparently the inspiration of Claude Perrault, designer of the Colonnade and the Observatory in Paris, and brother of Charles Perrault, creator of Mother Goose. In 1670 Perrault had the first 14 groups of children cast in lead after Lebrun sketches. In 1678 eight more groups were executed to decorate the halfmoon. In 1688 the 26 groups were replaced by bronze copies by Le Gros, Le Hongre, Lerambert, Mazeline and Buirette.

▲
THE WATER AVENUE
G NYMPHS

The Dragon Fountain

This pond is not visible from the North Parterre as it stands at the end of the Water Avenue. The center of the pond features a fountain with several figures (dolphins and cupids riding swans) encircling and fighting a dragon. The original sculptures by Marsy have been replaced by copies made in 1889. Under Louis XVI a water jet 90 feet high sprang from the mouth of the monster ; the jet was lowered to 35 feet when the fountains were in play during the king's absence.

THE DRAGON FOUNTAIN ▶

THE KING'S FAME,
◀ BY GUIDI

The Fountain of Neptune

Le Nôtre had planned for a fountain dedicated to Neptune in 1679 to complement the Dragon Fountain and the northern axis of the gardens (closed off by the sculpture by Guidi representing the King's Fame, counterpart of the Bernini statue to the south). But the Fountain of Neptune was only completed under Louis XV ; dug from 1678 to 1682, its design was slightly modified by Gabriel in 1738 making it possible for the structure to support (on top of the lead vases) the group depicting Neptune and Amphitrite. This group, by Lambert Sigisbert Adam (1741), is surrounded by the Ocean by Lemoine (1740) and Proteus, son of Neptune and god of the Sea by Bouchardon (1739). This fountain was inaugurated on August 14, 1741 by Louis XV ; its jets, 99 in all, are the finest at Versailles and provide the setting for the present Fêtes de Nuit held nowadays in summer.

▲
THE FOUNTAIN OF NEPTUNE
CENTER : NEPTUNE AND AMPHITRITE

▲
CUPID RIDING
A SEA DRAGON

TRIANON

Trianon was the name of the village bought by Louis XIV in 1668 to enlarge the grounds of Versailles. A pavilion was built here in 1670 by Levau, and was used for serving refreshments. The building was decorated with blue and white Delft-like porcelain and the pavilion was known as the Trianon de Porcelaine.

Though easy to maintain it fell into ruin and in 1687, the king decided to have it replaced by a real château where, if necessa-

ry, he could live, but only with his family (unlike Marly where certain privileged courtiers could be received). It was at that time that Hardouin-Mansart built the single-storey château, that we see today with its façades adorned with pilasters of Languedoc marble. Now known as the Grand Trianon, it had originally been called the Marble Trianon owing to its décor.

The design of the building is simple enough : on either side of the peristyle are two wings which can only be seen from the garden ; two projections close off the Royal Courtyard. From the righthand wing stretches a second wing, also decorated with Languedoc marble pilasters, from which stretches a third wing with two storeys, known as the Trianon-sous-Bois (Trianon-in-the-Woods) because of its sylvan setting. The inside of the Trianon was altered several times between 1688 and 1715. Originally, the king lived in the wing to the left, but had his apartment moved in 1703 to the fore-wing on the right, formerly a theater.

▲
ABOVE : FRONT GATE
◀ LEFT : PERISTYLE AND GALLER

He thus lived closer to his granddaughter, the duchess de Bourgogne (mother of Louis XV) and Madame de Maintenon, who occupied the right wing.

The Trianon was long neglected by Louis XV, but in 1750 he decided to have Madame de Maintenon's apartement redecorated for himself and Madame de Pompadour, the queen living in the Trianon-sous-Bois. He had a games room, a dining room and a buffet room set up in the fore-wing on the right where his ancestor had once lived. The Grand Trianon was merely an annex to the Petit Trianon under Louis XVI, and like all other royal residences was stripped of its furniture during the French Revolution. It was occupied once again under Napoleon, who had originally intended it for his mother, but moved in himself with his second wife, the archduchess Marie-Louise.

The Empress occupied the lefthand wing while the Emperor took up residence on the right, the wing retaining its 18th century configuration. Little used under the *Restauration,* (though Charles X held his last Council of Ministers here in 1830), the Grand Trianon was well liked by Louis-Philippe. He had a large family drawing room created in the right wing and, in the right fore-wing, an apartment for his daughter and her husband, the King and Queen of Belgium. Louis-Philippe and the queen lived in the left wing and often came to the Trianon while Versailles was being transformed into a museum.

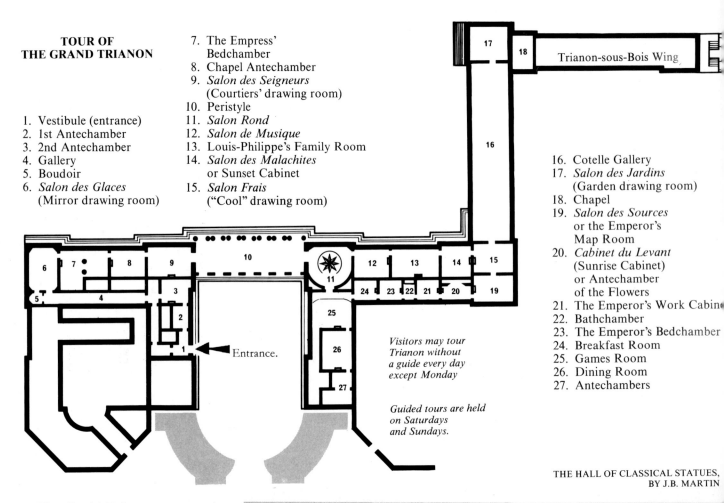

TOUR OF
THE GRAND TRIANON

1. Vestibule (entrance)
2. 1st Antechamber
3. 2nd Antechamber
4. Gallery
5. Boudoir
6. *Salon des Glaces*
   (Mirror drawing room)
7. The Empress'
   Bedchamber
8. Chapel Antechamber
9. *Salon des Seigneurs*
   (Courtiers' drawing room)
10. Peristyle
11. *Salon Rond*
12. *Salon de Musique*
13. Louis-Philippe's Family Room
14. *Salon des Malachites*
    or Sunset Cabinet
15. *Salon Frais*
    ("Cool" drawing room)

16. Cotelle Gallery
17. *Salon des Jardins*
    (Garden drawing room)
18. Chapel
19. *Salon des Sources*
    or the Emperor's
    Map Room
20. *Cabinet du Levant*
    (Sunrise Cabinet)
    or Antechamber
    of the Flowers
21. The Emperor's Work Cabinet
22. Bathchamber
23. The Emperor's Bedchamber
24. Breakfast Room
25. Games Room
26. Dining Room
27. Antechambers

*Visitors may tour
Trianon without
a guide every day
except Monday*

*Guided tours are held
on Saturdays
and Sundays.*

THE HALL OF CLASSICAL STATUES,
BY J.B. MARTIN

The Grand Trianon once again met with neglect under the Second Empire and the IIIrd and IVth Republics, and was only to be restored while de Gaulle was in office. Most of the paintings dating from the reign of the Sun King have been returned, but it is the Empire-style furnishings which have been brought back that provide the most satisfaction for those involved in the restoration of the building ; finally, the Family drawing room features some fine examples of Louis-Philippe furniture.

The gallery linking the right wing to the Trianon-sous-Bois is also known as the Cotelle Gallery, after the name of the artist whose works are embedded in the woodwork ; they are of particular interest as they portray the various groves of the gardens of Versailles and Trianon in the 17th century. The Trianon-sous-Bois wing housed the apartments of the Princes.

PRECEDING PAGE
ABOVE : THE EMPRESS'
BEDCHAMBER (LEFT WING)
◀ BELOW : THE SALON DES MALACHITES
(RIGHT WING)

The Gardens of the Grand Trianon

Here, as in all his châteaux, Louis XIV attached great importance to the gardens. The general layout remains that of the Trianon de Porcelaine, with an Upper Garden and a Lower Garden. Seven steps lead to the Upper Garden from the Peristyle ; the garden is made up of two parterres each with a pond in its center featuring a group of children, by Girardon.

Under Louis XIV the Lower Garden was planted with an abundance of orange trees and fragrant flowers. An octagonal pond is decorated with a sculpture by Marsy of a child surrounded by grapes ; an avenue leads straight ahead to the Mirror Fountain. To the south of the Lower Garden a balustrade overlooks the *Bassin du Fer à Cheval* (Horseshoe fountain), beyond which lies the north branch of the Grand Canal.

Hidden away behind the buildings and the foliage are several more parterres and fountains which add to the charm of the gardens (nonetheless neglected in the 18th and 19th centuries). The King's Garden lies in the angle formed by the fore-wing and the right wing of the Trianon ; between the Gallery and the Trianon-sous-Bois wing lies the former *Jardin des Sources* (Garden of the Springs), of which only remains one small pond and the name of one of Trianon's rooms, later used as a map room by Napoléon Bonaparte.

The gardens beyond the Trianon-sous-Bois have, however, preserved more of the fine decorative elements which Louis XIV had intended, and include the *Bassin à Oreilles* (Pool with two half-moons), the *Salle des Antiques* (Hall of Classical Statues), the *Salle Verte* (Green Hall) and, at the top of an avenue leading to the *Petite Etoile*, the famous Water Buffet built by Hardouin-Mansart. It is built in two shades of marble and is adorned with lead groups and reliefs by Mazière, Van Cleve, Le Lorrain, Poirier and Hardy.

▲
THE TIP OF THE GALLERY AND
THE SALON DES JARDINS

level (with a drop on two sides), a first storey and an attic storey surrounded by a balustrade. Each façade is decorated differently, the richest being the west front looking onto the French Garden with is high Corinthian-order columns.

The interior has largely remained as it did under Louis XV, and includes a vast *Salon de Compagnie* (reception room), dining room and staircase with its ornate wrought-iron banister. Upon his succession to the throne, Louis XVI presented the small château to his queen, Marie-Antoinette ; she had the *Cabinet de Travail*, or study, of her husband's grandfather converted into a bedchamber, and in place of a small staircase a private cabinet was built for her. By means of an ingenious device which has recently been repaired, the windows could be

THE PETIT TRIANON

Louis XV, like his great-grandfather Louis XIV, had been quite an expert on gardening, and from 1749 on had the northeast grounds of the Trianon laid out into what later became known as the Petit Trianon (Small Trianon).

The project was carried out in several stages. A new menagerie was built (the old one stood at the tip of the southern branch of the Grand Canal) ; then a new parterre, called the *Jardin Français* (French Garden), was designed, and in 1750 Gabriel had a small pavilion built in its center. Known as the *Pavillon Français*, or French Pavilion, it was accompanied by another small edifice, the Trellis Pavilion, recently reconstructed.

Further east, Louis XV had the botanist Bernard de Jussieu create a botanical garden, and put Claude Richard in charge of it. The garden, where fig trees, coffee trees, geraniums and strawberries had been cultivated, as well as the large hothouse built in 1767, did not survive. The *Bien-Aimé* (Louis XV) himself died in 1774 of smallpox ; the first symptoms had appeared while the king was staying in the new château built by Gabriel in 1761.

The Petit Trianon, built on a square ground plan, has a ground

▲
THE PETIT TRIANON

THE SALON DE COMPAGNIE ▶

92

covered up by "moving mirrors", and the room was known by this name. As in the château of Versailles, efforts are being made to refurnish these apartments in their original décor. Like Versailles, the Grand and Petit Trianons were stripped of their furniture during the Revolution. Redecorated by Napoleon Bonaparte for his sister Pauline Borghese, the Petit Trianon retains furnishings which are more similar to those of the Grand Trianon under Louis XVIII (when the duc and duchesse de Berry lived there) and, in particular, under Louis-Philippe when the crown prince and princess, the duc and duchesse d'Orléans, lived there. In 1867 Empress Eugénie, a great admirer of Marie-Antoinette, organized an exhibition to honor the queen, thus providing the first effort to restore the Petit Trianon in the Louis XVI style, an effort still maintained to this day.

The Gardens of the Petit Trianon and the Queen's Hamlet

There is no doubt that when Marie-Antoinette received the Petit Trianon and its grounds as a gift from Louis XVI, the gardens, which had been designed for the purpose of studying botany, could be of little if no interest to a queen so taken up with the latest fashions and, in this case, English-style gardens.

The queen had the rare plants transferred to the King's Garden in Paris, and asked Hubert Robert and the architect Mique to redesign the gardens of her little domain. This is when the quaint scenery, with its green lawns and rivulets which still delight visitors today, was created. The buildings were constructed progressively, often following the queen's whims, or fashions she followed or created herself.

In 1777 Mique built an octagonal pavilion, the Belvedere, on a rock overlooking the lake. Its interior was decorated with stuccos by Le Riche under a domed roof painted by Lagrenée. A small classical temple, visible from the queen's bed-

THE BELVEDERE ▲
THE TEMPLE OF LOVE ▶

chamber, was built on an island. It is known as the Temple of Love because of the statue of Cupid, by Bouchard, which stands in its center.

In 1780 Mique built a theater for Marie-Antoinette, who thought nothing of appearing on stage herself in such scandalous productions as "The Marriage of Figaro" by Beaumarchais. In fact only the Royal Family attended the performances and the theater, hidden away among the trees, is harmoniously decorated in blue and gold finery similar to the Opera in the château.

But it was the Hamlet which made the Queen's Garden famous. Like Madame de Lamballe at Rambouillet and the Condé at Chantilly, Marie-Antoinette wanted a village of her own whose houses, modelled after cottages in Normandy, in fact contained drawing rooms of considerable elegance. Twelve houses were originally built by Mique from 1783 to 1785 ; ten of these still stand today and include the Queen's Cottage, the Mill and, near the Dairy, the fishery tower also known as the Marlborough Tower, after a French song "Marlbrouk s'en va-t'en guerre" (Marlborough going off to war) made famous by the Dauphin's wetnurse, Madame Poitrine.

The Musée des Voitures, built between the Grand and Petit Trianons in the 19th century, has recently been transferred to the Grande Ecurie in front of the château. Work is in progress and the collection of old "berlin" carriages used by Napoléon, as well as Charles X's coronation carriage, purchased by Louis-Philippe to complete his museum commemorating France's glory, will shortly be open to the public.

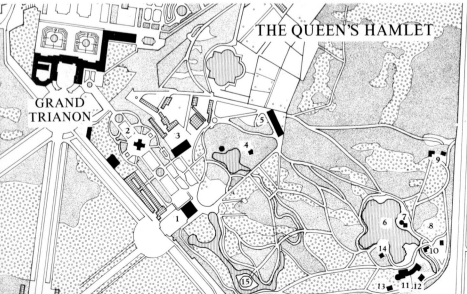

THE QUEEN'S HAMLET

GRAND TRIANON

1. *The Petit Trianon*
2. *The French Pavilion and the Trellis Pavilion*
3. *The Theater*
4. *The Small Lake, Belvedere and Grotto*
5. *The Orangery of Trianon*
6. *The Great Lake and the Hamlet*
7. *The Fishery and the Dairy*
8. *The Ballroom*
9. *The Farm*
10. *The Dovecot*
11. *The Queen's Cottage* ▶
12. *The Réchauffoir*
13. *The Boudoir*
14. *The Mill*
15. *The Temple of Love*

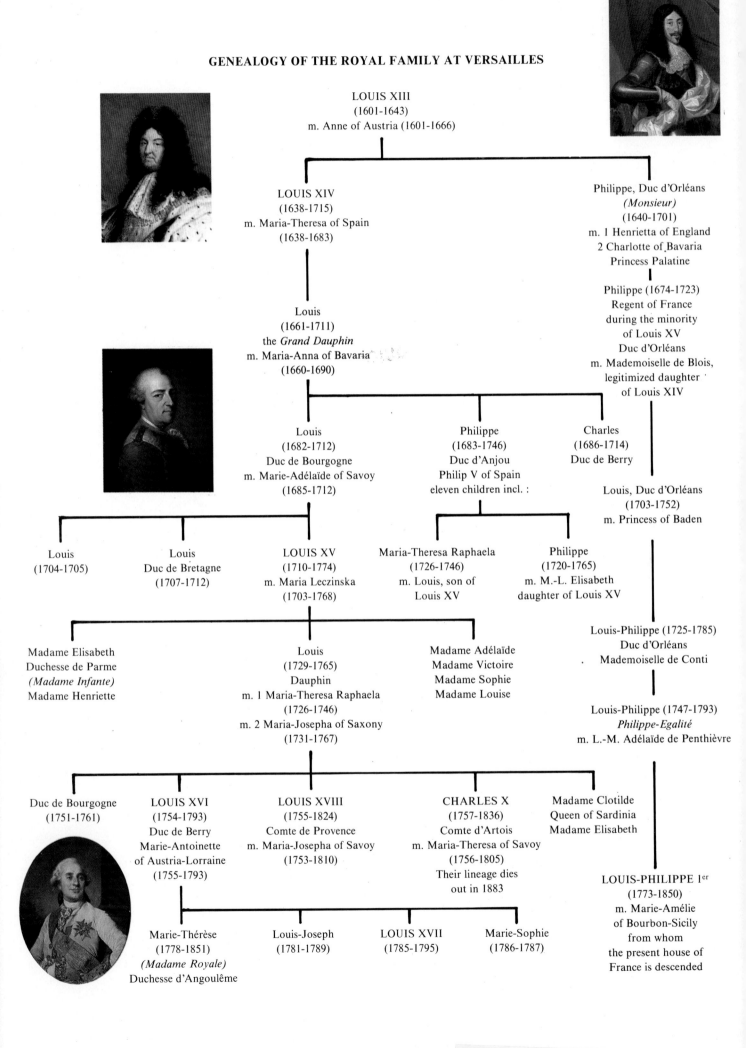

LOUIS XIII
(1601-1643)
m. Anne of Austria (1601-1666)

LOUIS XIV
(1638-1715)
m. Maria-Theresa of Spain
(1638-1683)

Philippe, Duc d'Orléans
(Monsieur)
(1640-1701)
m. 1 Henrietta of England
2 Charlotte of Bavaria
Princess Palatine

Louis
(1661-1711)
the Grand Dauphin
m. Maria-Anna of Bavaria
(1660-1690)

Philippe (1674-1723)
Regent of France
during the minority
of Louis XV
Duc d'Orléans
m. Mademoiselle de Blois,
legitimized daughter
of Louis XIV

Louis
(1682-1712)
Duc de Bourgogne
m. Marie-Adélaïde of Savoy
(1685-1712)

Philippe
(1683-1746)
Duc d'Anjou
Philip V of Spain
eleven children incl. :

Charles
(1686-1714)
Duc de Berry

Louis, Duc d'Orléans
(1703-1752)
m. Princess of Baden

Louis
(1704-1705)

Louis
Duc de Bretagne
(1707-1712)

LOUIS XV
(1710-1774)
m. Maria Leczinska
(1703-1768)

Maria-Theresa Raphaela
(1726-1746)
m. Louis, son of
Louis XV

Philippe
(1720-1765)
m. M.-L. Elisabeth
daughter of Louis XV

Louis-Philippe (1725-1785)
Duc d'Orléans
Mademoiselle de Conti

Madame Elisabeth
Duchesse de Parme
(Madame Infante)
Madame Henriette

Louis
(1729-1765)
Dauphin
m. 1 Maria-Theresa Raphaela
(1726-1746)
m. 2 Maria-Josepha of Saxony
(1731-1767)

Madame Adélaïde
Madame Victoire
Madame Sophie
Madame Louise

Louis-Philippe (1747-1793)
Philippe-Egalité
m. L.-M. Adélaïde de Penthièvre

Duc de Bourgogne
(1751-1761)

LOUIS XVI
(1754-1793)
Duc de Berry
Marie-Antoinette
of Austria-Lorraine
(1755-1793)

LOUIS XVIII
(1755-1824)
Comte de Provence
m. Maria-Josepha of Savoy
(1753-1810)

CHARLES X
(1757-1836)
Comte d'Artois
m. Maria-Theresa of Savoy
(1756-1805)
Their lineage dies
out in 1883

Madame Clotilde
Queen of Sardinia
Madame Elisabeth

LOUIS-PHILIPPE Ier
(1773-1850)
m. Marie-Amélie
of Bourbon-Sicily
from whom
the present house of
France is descended

Marie-Thérèse
(1778-1851)
(Madame Royale)
Duchesse d'Angoulême

Louis-Joseph
(1781-1789)

LOUIS XVII
(1785-1795)

Marie-Sophie
(1786-1787)